The 1997 STAR TREK® Diary
Designed and Edited by George Papadeas

First published in Australasia in 1996 by
Simon & Schuster Australia
20 Barcoo Street
East Roseville NSW 2069

First published in Great Britain in 1996 by
Simon & Schuster Limited
West Garden Place, Kendal Street
London W2 2AQ

Viacom International
Sydney New York London Toronto Tokyo Singapore

TM, ® & © 1996 Paramount Pictures. All Rights Reserved.
STAR TREK and Related Marks are Trademarks of Paramount Pictures.
Simon & Schuster Australia Authorised User.

All rights reserved. No part of this publication may be reproduced, stored in a retrieval system, or transmitted, in any form or by any means, electronic, mechanical, photocopying, recording, or otherwise, without the prior permission of the copyright holder in writing.

ISBN: 0 671 85575 1

Printed in Hong Kong by South China Printing Co (1988) Ltd

For more information on STAR TREK®, contact:

GPO Box 2067 Sydney 2001 Australia
Telephone: (61 2) 9311 3841
Facsimile: (61 2) 9311 3607

The 1997 STAR TREK® DIARY

POCKET BOOKS

1997/1998 CALENDARS

1997

JANUARY
M	T	W	T	F	S	S
		1	2	3	4	5
6	7	8	9	10	11	12
13	14	15	16	17	18	19
20	21	22	23	24	25	26
27	28	29	30	31		

FEBRUARY
M	T	W	T	F	S	S
					1	2
3	4	5	6	7	8	9
10	11	12	13	14	15	16
17	18	19	20	21	22	23
24	25	26	27	28		

MARCH
M	T	W	T	F	S	S
31					1	2
3	4	5	6	7	8	9
10	11	12	13	14	15	16
17	18	19	20	21	22	23
24	25	26	27	28	29	30

APRIL
M	T	W	T	F	S	S
	1	2	3	4	5	6
7	8	9	10	11	12	13
14	15	16	17	18	19	20
21	22	23	24	25	26	27
28	29	30				

MAY
M	T	W	T	F	S	S
			1	2	3	4
5	6	7	8	9	10	11
12	13	14	15	16	17	18
19	20	21	22	23	24	25
26	27	28	29	30	31	

JUNE
M	T	W	T	F	S	S
30						1
2	3	4	5	6	7	8
9	10	11	12	13	14	15
16	17	18	19	20	21	22
23	24	25	26	27	28	29

JULY
M	T	W	T	F	S	S
	1	2	3	4	5	6
7	8	9	10	11	12	13
14	15	16	17	18	19	20
21	22	23	24	25	26	27
28	29	30	31			

AUGUST
M	T	W	T	F	S	S
				1	2	3
4	5	6	7	8	9	10
11	12	13	14	15	16	17
18	19	20	21	22	23	24
25	26	27	28	29	30	31

SEPTEMBER
M	T	W	T	F	S	S
1	2	3	4	5	6	7
8	9	10	11	12	13	14
15	16	17	18	19	20	21
22	23	24	25	26	27	28
29	30					

OCTOBER
M	T	W	T	F	S	S
		1	2	3	4	5
6	7	8	9	10	11	12
13	14	15	16	17	18	19
20	21	22	23	24	25	26
27	28	29	30	31		

NOVEMBER
M	T	W	T	F	S	S
					1	2
3	4	5	6	7	8	9
10	11	12	13	14	15	16
17	18	19	20	21	22	23
24	25	26	27	28	29	30

DECEMBER
M	T	W	T	F	S	S
29	30	31				
1	2	3	4	5	6	7
8	9	10	11	12	13	14
15	16	17	18	19	20	21
22	23	24	25	26	27	28

1998

JANUARY
M	T	W	T	F	S	S
			1	2	3	4
5	6	7	8	9	10	11
12	13	14	15	16	17	18
19	20	21	22	23	24	25
26	27	28	29	30	31	

FEBRUARY
M	T	W	T	F	S	S
						1
2	3	4	5	6	7	8
9	10	11	12	13	14	15
16	17	18	19	20	21	22
23	24	25	26	27	28	

MARCH
M	T	W	T	F	S	S
30	31					1
2	3	4	5	6	7	8
9	10	11	12	13	14	15
16	17	18	19	20	21	22
23	24	25	26	27	28	29

APRIL
M	T	W	T	F	S	S
		1	2	3	4	5
6	7	8	9	10	11	12
13	14	15	16	17	18	19
20	21	22	23	24	25	26
27	28	29	30			

MAY
M	T	W	T	F	S	S
				1	2	3
4	5	6	7	8	9	10
11	12	13	14	15	16	17
18	19	20	21	22	23	24
25	26	27	28	29	30	31

JUNE
M	T	W	T	F	S	S
1	2	3	4	5	6	7
8	9	10	11	12	13	14
15	16	17	18	19	20	21
22	23	24	25	26	27	28
29	30					

JULY
M	T	W	T	F	S	S
		1	2	3	4	5
6	7	8	9	10	11	12
13	14	15	16	17	18	19
20	21	22	23	24	25	26
27	28	29	30	31		

AUGUST
M	T	W	T	F	S	S
31					1	2
3	4	5	6	7	8	9
10	11	12	13	14	15	16
17	18	19	20	21	22	23
24	25	26	27	28	29	30

SEPTEMBER
M	T	W	T	F	S	S
	1	2	3	4	5	6
7	8	9	10	11	12	13
14	15	16	17	18	19	20
21	22	23	24	25	26	27
28	29	30				

OCTOBER
M	T	W	T	F	S	S
			1	2	3	4
5	6	7	8	9	10	11
12	13	14	15	16	17	18
19	20	21	22	23	24	25
26	27	28	29	30	31	

NOVEMBER
M	T	W	T	F	S	S
30						1
2	3	4	5	6	7	8
9	10	11	12	13	14	15
16	17	18	19	20	21	22
23	24	25	26	27	28	29

DECEMBER
M	T	W	T	F	S	S
	1	2	3	4	5	6
7	8	9	10	11	12	13
14	15	16	17	18	19	20
21	22	23	24	25	26	27
28	29	30	31			

◖ CREW MANIFEST

Name _____

Home Planet Address _____

_____ Coordinates _____

Crew Number _____ Fax _____

Starfleet Rank _____ Starship _____

Chief Medical Officer _____

Chief Dental Officer _____

Emergency Contact at Starfleet Command _____

Shuttlecraft Insurance Policy Number _____

Shuttlecraft Insurance Due _____

Galactic Space Service Number _____

MOST FREQUENT COORDINATES

Name	Coordinates
_____	_____
_____	_____
_____	_____
_____	_____
_____	_____
_____	_____
_____	_____
_____	_____

311 3841
311 3607
NCC 1701
956 5000
1800
671701
190257

IMPORTANT STARDATES

Stardate	Stardate
_____	_____
_____	_____
_____	_____
_____	_____
_____	_____
_____	_____

956
500
362
243
600
311

GENE RODDENBERRY – *STAR TREK* CREATOR

Gene Roddenberry showed uncanny vision when he developed the futuristic show STAR TREK, a phenomenon that continues to enchant to this day.

After his great service in creating STAR TREK, Gene Roddenberry was honoured with a star on Hollywood's *walk of fame* in 1985.

Later he inaugurated STAR TREK: THE NEXT GENERATION, proving that lightning can indeed strike twice.

DECEMBER						1996		JANUARY						1997		FEBRUARY						1997
M	T	W	T	F	S	S		M	T	W	T	F	S	S		M	T	W	T	F	S	S
30	31					1				1	2	3	4	5							1	2
2	3	4	5	6	7	8		6	7	8	9	10	11	12		3	4	5	6	7	8	9
9	10	11	12	13	14	15		13	14	15	16	17	18	19		10	11	12	13	14	15	16
16	17	18	19	20	21	22		20	21	22	23	24	25	26		17	18	19	20	21	22	23
23	24	25	26	27	28	29		27	28	29	30	31				24	25	26	27	28		

DECEMBER-JANUARY

MONDAY 30

New Year's Eve

TUESDAY 31

New Year's Day

WEDNESDAY 1

Holiday (Scotland)
Day After New Year's Day (New Zealand)

THURSDAY 2

FRIDAY 3

SATURDAY 4

SUNDAY 5

1997 – 10 YEARS OF STAR TREK: THE NEXT GENERATION

Following the very successful fourth feature film STAR TREK IV: THE VOYAGE HOME, PARAMOUNT commissioned Gene Roddenberry to create an extension of the STAR TREK world.

Utilising many of his original series creators, Roddenberry set about producing STAR TREK: THE NEXT GENERATION, which premiered in September 1987. The show went on for seven very successful seasons, creating a modern day ratings phenomenon, which spawned two other series. Ten years later, STAR TREK: THE NEXT GENERATION is still popular, and continues to enjoy healthy re-run ratings.

The crew of STAR TREK: THE NEXT GENERATION.
From left: Lt Cmdr Geordi La Forge, Counsellor Deana Troi, Lt Cmdr Data, Captain Picard, Lt Worf, Dr Crusher, Commander Riker.

DECEMBER						1996		JANUARY						1997		FEBRUARY						1997
M	T	W	T	F	S	S		M	T	W	T	F	S	S		M	T	W	T	F	S	S
30	31					1				1	2	3	4	5							1	2
2	3	4	5	6	7	8		6	7	8	9	10	11	12		3	4	5	6	7	8	9
9	10	11	12	13	14	15		13	14	15	16	17	18	19		10	11	12	13	14	15	16
16	17	18	19	20	21	22		20	21	22	23	24	25	26		17	18	19	20	21	22	23
23	24	25	26	27	28	29		27	28	29	30	31				24	25	26	27	28		

JANUARY

Epiphany (Germany)

MONDAY 6

TUESDAY 7

WEDNESDAY 8

THURSDAY 9

FRIDAY 10

SATURDAY 11

SUNDAY 12

CAPTAIN JEAN-LUC PICARD

The captain of the U.S.S. Enterprise NCC-1701-D is hardened space veteran, Jean-Luc Picard.

Played by Shakespearean actor Patrick Stewart, the charismatic role became the cornerstone for the success of STAR TREK: THE NEXT GENERATION. Blessed with a superb voice, and classical acting skills, Stewart added a new dimension to the perception of Starfleet Captain.

From the first episode, "Encounter At Farpoint", to the final, "All Good Things...", Captain Picard easily handled the challenges.

DECEMBER						1996	JANUARY						1997	FEBRUARY						1997
M	T	W	T	F	S	S	M	T	W	T	F	S	S	M	T	W	T	F	S	S
30	31					1			1	2	3	4	5						1	2
2	3	4	5	6	7	8	6	7	8	9	10	11	12	3	4	5	6	7	8	9
9	10	11	12	13	14	15	13	14	15	16	17	18	19	10	11	12	13	14	15	16
16	17	18	19	20	21	22	20	21	22	23	24	25	26	17	18	19	20	21	22	23
23	24	25	26	27	28	29	27	28	29	30	31			24	25	26	27	28		

 **JANUARY**

MONDAY 13

TUESDAY 14

Coming-Of-Age Day (Seijin-No Hi, Japan)

WEDNESDAY 15

THURSDAY 16

FRIDAY 17

SATURDAY 18

SUNDAY 19

COMMANDER WILLIAM T. RIKER, FIRST OFFICER

The consummate first officer, Riker has quickly established himself as worthy of one day commanding his own ship. Indeed he is famous for rejecting several command offers from Starfleet, instead preferring to serve on board the *Starship Enterprise*.

His easy-going nature belies the fact that he takes his command seriously, and is a very competent first officer, overlooking all staffing decisions on board the ship.

Played to perfection by Jonathan Frakes, who instills some of his own personality in the character, Riker has become one of the most dependable of all crew members.

Frakes has also left his mark on the continuing STAR TREK legend by becoming one of the series' favourite directors. He has directed both STAR TREK: DEEP SPACE NINE and STAR TREK: VOYAGER. His latest assignment has been the eighth STAR TREK feature film, STAR TREK: FIRST CONTACT.

DECEMBER					1996			JANUARY					1997			FEBRUARY					1997	
M	T	W	T	F	S	S	M	T	W	T	F	S	S	M	T	W	T	F	S	S		
30	31					1			1	2	3	4	5						1	2		
2	3	4	5	6	7	8	6	7	8	9	10	11	12	3	4	5	6	7	8	9		
9	10	11	12	13	14	15	13	14	15	16	17	18	19	10	11	12	13	14	15	16		
16	17	18	19	20	21	22	20	21	22	23	24	25	26	17	18	19	20	21	22	23		
23	24	25	26	27	28	29	27	28	29	30	31			24	25	26	27	28				

JANUARY

DeForest Kelley's Birthday (Dr Leonard 'Bones' McCoy)

Martin Luther King Jr Day (USA)

MONDAY 20

TUESDAY 21

WEDNESDAY 22

THURSDAY 23

FRIDAY 24

SATURDAY 25

SUNDAY 26

DANGEROUS ALIEN CULTURES

The first encounter with the Borg, "Q, Who", proved to be a very dangerous and inequitable meeting. The *U.S.S. Enterprise*, and her crew, were lucky to survive knowing that other deadly and challenging encounters were soon to follow.

Dealing with the collective nature of the Borg is one of the more difficult assignments to be undertaken by the Federation.

Another awkward adversary is the Romulan Empire. Though not as constant a threat as in the past, Romulans are still dangerous when backed into a corner. Here Picard is seen dealing with Tallera (Robin Curtis - who also played Lieutenant Saavik in STAR TREK III: THE SEARCH FOR SPOCK and STAR TREK IV: THE VOYAGE HOME), who is actually a Vulcan masquerading as a Romulan, in the episodes "The Gambit, Parts I & II".

DECEMBER						1996		JANUARY						1997		FEBRUARY						1997
M	T	W	T	F	S	S		M	T	W	T	F	S	S		M	T	W	T	F	S	S
30	31					1				1	2	3	4	5							1	2
2	3	4	5	6	7	8		6	7	8	9	10	11	12		3	4	5	6	7	8	9
9	10	11	12	13	14	15		13	14	15	16	17	18	19		10	11	12	13	14	15	16
16	17	18	19	20	21	22		20	21	22	23	24	25	26		17	18	19	20	21	22	23
23	24	25	26	27	28	29		27	28	29	30	31				24	25	26	27	28		

JANUARY-FEBRUARY

Australia Day (Australia)

MONDAY 27

TUESDAY 28

WEDNESDAY 29

THURSDAY 30

FRIDAY 31

SATURDAY 1

Brent Spiner's Birthday (Lieutenant Commander Data)

SUNDAY 2

PICARD ENCOUNTERS

Above: In the episode "Attached", Captain Jean-Luc Picard and Dr Beverly Crusher finally discuss their relationship in a very open and honest way. It seems that Jean-Luc was harbouring a secret affection for Beverly, and was troubled by these feelings when his best friend, Jack Crusher, married Beverly.

The relationship was further complicated when Jack Crusher was killed while on a mission with Picard. Still very much in love with Beverly, he stayed away out of honour and respect for his fallen friend.

It is only after a Louin mind device was used, that Beverly became aware of Jean-Luc's feelings.

Right: In "Preemptive Strike", Picard once again gives Ro Laren the benefit of the doubt, only to be betrayed. Instead of infiltrating the Maquis, Ro leaves Starfleet and joins the Maquis.

JANUARY						1997		FEBRUARY						1997		MARCH						1997
M	T	W	T	F	S	S		M	T	W	T	F	S	S		M	T	W	T	F	S	S
		1	2	3	4	5							1	2		31					1	2
6	7	8	9	10	11	12		3	4	5	6	7	8	9		3	4	5	6	7	8	9
13	14	15	16	17	18	19		10	11	12	13	14	15	16		10	11	12	13	14	15	16
20	21	22	23	24	25	26		17	18	19	20	21	22	23		17	18	19	20	21	22	23
27	28	29	30	31				24	25	26	27	28				24	25	26	27	28	29	30

 **FEBRUARY**

MONDAY **3**

TUESDAY **4**

WEDNESDAY **5**

Waitangi Day (New Zealand)

THURSDAY **6**

FRIDAY **7**

Ethan Phillip's Birthday (Neelix)

SATURDAY **8**

SUNDAY **9**

COUNSELLOR DEANNA TROI

Left: Ship's counsellor is Deanna Troi. Her role is to ensure that any psychological problems that confront the crew are handled swiftly and efficiently.

Her telepathic powers have also been invaluable to Captain Picard during tense situations on the bridge of the *U.S.S. Enterprise*.

Below: In "The Masterpiece Society", a long lost Earth colony which has been genetically engineered to be a "perfect society". They feel only by maintaining the status quo can they preserve their perfect society. While Counsellor Troi tries to persuade the colony's leader to consider relocation, the rest of the crew try to save the colony.

JANUARY					1997			FEBRUARY					1997			MARCH					1997	
M	T	W	T	F	S	S		M	T	W	T	F	S	S		M	T	W	T	F	S	S
		1	2	3	4	5							1	2		31					1	2
6	7	8	9	10	11	12		3	4	5	6	7	8	9		3	4	5	6	7	8	9
13	14	15	16	17	18	19		10	11	12	13	14	15	16		10	11	12	13	14	15	16
20	21	22	23	24	25	26		17	18	19	20	21	22	23		17	18	19	20	21	22	23
27	28	29	30	31				24	25	26	27	28				24	25	26	27	28	29	30

FEBRUARY

Rosenmontag (Germany) — **MONDAY 10**

National Foundation Day (Kenkoku-No-Hi, Japan) — **TUESDAY 11**

Abraham Lincoln's Birthday (USA) — **WEDNESDAY 12**
Susan Oliver's Birthday (Vina)

THURSDAY 13

St Valentine's Day — **FRIDAY 14**

SATURDAY 15

LeVar Burton's Birthday (Lieutenant Commander Geordi La Forge)

SUNDAY 16

Ash Wednesday (Australia)

DOCTOR BEVERLY CRUSHER

Above: Chief Medical Officer aboard the *U.S.S. Enterprise* is Dr Beverly Crusher. Despite having a difficult past with Captain Picard, she requested this assignment, and has proven to be a valuable part of the crew.

Crusher holds the rank of commander. She has commanded the ship in Picard's absence, and shows her mettle in command.

Though medicine is her passion, she also has to cope with her brilliant son Wesley as he finds his place aboard the ship.

Right: In "Data's Day", Beverly takes time out to show Data the finer points of dancing, as he prepares for Keiko and Chief O'Brien's wedding. As is often the case, Data's rapid learning and memory skills give the "dancing doctor" an apt pupil.

JANUARY						1997		FEBRUARY						1997		MARCH						1997
M	T	W	T	F	S	S		M	T	W	T	F	S	S		M	T	W	T	F	S	S
		1	2	3	4	5							1	2		31					1	2
6	7	8	9	10	11	12		3	4	5	6	7	8	9		3	4	5	6	7	8	9
13	14	15	16	17	18	19		10	11	12	13	14	15	16		10	11	12	13	14	15	16
20	21	22	23	24	25	26		17	18	19	20	21	22	23		17	18	19	20	21	22	23
27	28	29	30	31				24	25	26	27	28				24	25	26	27	28	29	30

◀ FEBRUARY

President's Day (USA) — **MONDAY 17**

TUESDAY 18

WEDNESDAY 19

THURSDAY 20

FRIDAY 21

George Washington's Birthday (USA) — **SATURDAY 22**
Majel Barrett's Birthday (Nurse Chapel, Lwaxana Troi, ship's computer voice)

SUNDAY 23

THE BEAT OF THE WARP ENGINES

Chief Engineer Geordi La Forge's heart beats to the same rhythm as the warp engines of the massive Galaxy-Class *U.S.S. Enterprise*.

Despite having a visual impairment, with the aid of his VISOR (Visual Information Sensory Output Recorder), he was able to rise to the task as chief engineer. The VISOR is able to pick up normally invisible sections of the electromagnetic spectrum.

Throughout the seven-year run of STAR TREK: THE NEXT GENERATION, La Forge was able to keep the warp engines operational.

In the film STAR TREK GENERATIONS, not even his great skill could prevent the final and terrifying warp core breach that destroyed the star-drive section of the ship.

FEBRUARY						1997		MARCH						1997		APRIL						1997
M	T	W	T	F	S	S		M	T	W	T	F	S	S		M	T	W	T	F	S	S
					1	2		31					1	2			1	2	3	4	5	6
3	4	5	6	7	8	9		3	4	5	6	7	8	9		7	8	9	10	11	12	13
10	11	12	13	14	15	16		10	11	12	13	14	15	16		14	15	16	17	18	19	20
17	18	19	20	21	22	23		17	18	19	20	21	22	23		21	22	23	24	25	26	27
24	25	26	27	28				24	25	26	27	28	29	30		28	29	30				

FEBRUARY-MARCH

MONDAY 24

TUESDAY 25

WEDNESDAY 26

THURSDAY 27

FRIDAY 28

St David's Day (Wales) — **SATURDAY 1**

SUNDAY 2

THE PASSAGE OF TIME

Above: The one overriding factor in the success of the original STAR TREK series, was the chemistry between the characters created by skilled actors. In the very popular episode "City On The Edge Of Forever", the interplay between Kirk and Spock is especially poignant considering the choice Spock knows Kirk must make.

Below left: Kirk and Spock have an interesting adventure when they reach the planet of the Iotians, who have modelled their society on a book from the Chicago mobsters era – left by a passing starship.

Below centre: Spock plays a central role in "Is There In Truth No Beauty", an episode notable in that Dian Muldaur starred. She also played in the other original series episode, "Return To Tomorrow". Muldaur then went on to become the chief medical officer in the second season of STAR TREK: THE NEXT GENERATION.

Below right: In the unprecedented second pilot "Where No Man Has Gone Before", Kirk and Spock concur on how to handle the 'espers' (crew members with heightened ESP capabilities, created by passing through the energy rim of the galaxy).

FEBRUARY						1997		MARCH						1997		APRIL						1997
M	T	W	T	F	S	S		M	T	W	T	F	S	S		M	T	W	T	F	S	S
					1	2		31					1	2			1	2	3	4	5	6
3	4	5	6	7	8	9		3	4	5	6	7	8	9		7	8	9	10	11	12	13
10	11	12	13	14	15	16		10	11	12	13	14	15	16		14	15	16	17	18	19	20
17	18	19	20	21	22	23		17	18	19	20	21	22	23		21	22	23	24	25	26	27
24	25	26	27	28				24	25	26	27	28	29	30		28	29	30				

◀ MARCH ▶

James Doohan's Birthday (Chief Engineer Montgomery Scott)

MONDAY 3

TUESDAY 4

WEDNESDAY 5

THURSDAY 6

FRIDAY 7

SATURDAY 8

Mothering Sunday (UK)

SUNDAY 9

CHIEF MEDICAL OFFICER, DR LEONARD McCOY

Dr Leonard 'Bones' McCoy is the acerbic chief medical officer aboard the *U.S.S. Enterprise*. His role is vital in the day-to-day running of the starship. His duties are many and varied, particularly when alien civilisations are encountered. One such event involved a race of beings travelling to a pre-ordained destination aboard a vessel that they perceived as being a planet. In this episode, "For The World Is Hollow And I Have Touched The Sky", McCoy diagnoses himself as being terminally ill. After falling in love with the high priestess, Natira, he gets access to their medical records, where it is discovered there is a cure for his illness.

Above: In the episode "Shore Leave", McCoy and Yeoman Barrows become participants in their own fantasies, courtesy of the planet's computer system. He is the "Prince Charming", and she is the "fair maiden".

FEBRUARY						1997		MARCH						1997		APRIL						1997
M	T	W	T	F	S	S		M	T	W	T	F	S	S		M	T	W	T	F	S	S
					1	2		31					1	2			1	2	3	4	5	6
3	4	5	6	7	8	9		3	4	5	6	7	8	9		7	8	9	10	11	12	13
10	11	12	13	14	15	16		10	11	12	13	14	15	16		14	15	16	17	18	19	20
17	18	19	20	21	22	23		17	18	19	20	21	22	23		21	22	23	24	25	26	27
24	25	26	27	28				24	25	26	27	28	29	30		28	29	30				

 **MARCH**

MONDAY **10**

TUESDAY **11**

WEDNESDAY **12**

THURSDAY **13**

FRIDAY **14**

SATURDAY **15**

SUNDAY **16**

THE KLINGON EMPIRE

Above: In "Day Of The Dove", Kirk does battle with the Klingon Commander Kang. An alien entity that feeds off the energy of conflict goads Kang and Kirk to fight while trapped together aboard the *U.S.S. Enterprise*. Only after Kirk discovers this, he persuades Kang to stop the combat.

Below: The Organians imposed a peace treaty on the Federation and the Klingon Empire. They were a lifeform so evolved that they had no need for bodies. Once drawn into the conflict they found both societies' violence abhorrent.

FEBRUARY						1997		MARCH						1997		APRIL						1997
M	T	W	T	F	S	S		M	T	W	T	F	S	S		M	T	W	T	F	S	S
					1	2		31					1	2			1	2	3	4	5	6
3	4	5	6	7	8	9		3	4	5	6	7	8	9		7	8	9	10	11	12	13
10	11	12	13	14	15	16		10	11	12	13	14	15	16		14	15	16	17	18	19	20
17	18	19	20	21	22	23		17	18	19	20	21	22	23		21	22	23	24	25	26	27
24	25	26	27	28				24	25	26	27	28	29	30		28	29	30				

 **MARCH**

St Patrick's Day (Ireland)   **MONDAY 17**

TUESDAY 18

WEDNESDAY 19

Vernal Equinox Day   **THURSDAY 20**

Human Rights Day (South Africa)   **FRIDAY 21**

William Shatner's Birthday (Captain James T. Kirk)

SATURDAY 22

Palm Sunday   **SUNDAY 23**

THE ONGOING MISSION...

Left: In "What Are Little Girls Made Of?", Kirk and Chapel beam down to communicate with the long-lost scientist, Dr Roger Korby, Nurse Chapel's fiancée. Dr Korby has been missing for five years. While on the planet during this time, he has developed the "ultimate" android.

To prove his sanity to Kirk and Chapel, Korby manufactures a duplicate Kirk. As time progresses, it becomes apparent that he is a very disturbed man. Korby has lost himself in his pursuit of science, leaving his humanity behind.

On September 8, 1966, STAR TREK premiered in the US on the NBC network. After two pilots ("The Cage" in 1964 and "Where No Man Has Gone Before" in 1965), with two different crews, the adventure was now beginning. With about six episodes in the can, the network chose "The Man Trap" (below), the sixth in the series filmed to launch Gene Roddenberry's futuristic vision.

The episode was considered a "good mix" of morality and adventure. This episode launched the show on a rocky and turbulent three-year life on network television. It was only after syndication that STAR TREK became universally popular. It is translated into over one hundred different languages, for all the world to appreciate and enjoy.

FEBRUARY						1997	MARCH						1997	APRIL						1997
M	T	W	T	F	S	S	M	T	W	T	F	S	S	M	T	W	T	F	S	S
					1	2	31					1	2		1	2	3	4	5	6
3	4	5	6	7	8	9	3	4	5	6	7	8	9	7	8	9	10	11	12	13
10	11	12	13	14	15	16	10	11	12	13	14	15	16	14	15	16	17	18	19	20
17	18	19	20	21	22	23	17	18	19	20	21	22	23	21	22	23	24	25	26	27
24	25	26	27	28			24	25	26	27	28	29	30	28	29	30				

MARCH

MONDAY 24

TUESDAY 25

Leonard Nimoy's Birthday (Mr Spock)

WEDNESDAY 26

THURSDAY 27

Good Friday

FRIDAY 28

Marina Sirtis's Birthday (Counsellor Deanna Troi)

Easter Saturday

SATURDAY 29

Easter Sunday
British Summer Time begins

SUNDAY 30

VULCAN VALUES

Above: In the episode "Mirror, Mirror", the alternative universe Spock and our Dr McCoy continue to build on one of STAR TREK's most enduring relationships. Their constant crossing of wits is one of the highlights of the original series.

Below: Spock's parents, Sarek, his Vulcan father, and Amanda, his human mother, come aboard the U.S.S. *Enterprise* in "Journey To Babel". Sarek, the Vulcan ambassador, has not spoken to his son as a father in over fifteen years. Amanda hopes the trip will heal the rift.

MARCH						1997		APRIL						1997		MAY						1997
M	T	W	T	F	S	S		M	T	W	T	F	S	S		M	T	W	T	F	S	S
31					1	2			1	2	3	4	5	6					1	2	3	4
3	4	5	6	7	8	9		7	8	9	10	11	12	13		5	6	7	8	9	10	11
10	11	12	13	14	15	16		14	15	16	17	18	19	20		12	13	14	15	16	17	18
17	18	19	20	21	22	23		21	22	23	24	25	26	27		19	20	21	22	23	24	25
24	25	26	27	28	29	30		28	29	30						26	27	28	29	30	31	

MARCH-APRIL

Easter Monday — **MONDAY 31**

Grace Lee Whitney's Birthday (Yeoman Janice Rand)

April Fools' Day — **TUESDAY 1**

WEDNESDAY 2

THURSDAY 3

FRIDAY 4

SATURDAY 5

SUNDAY 6

CHIEF ENGINEER, MONTGOMERY SCOTT

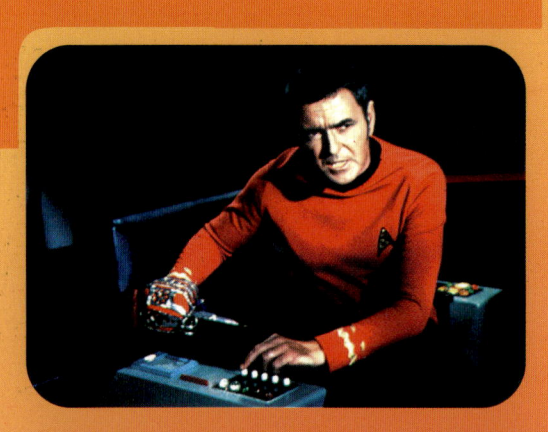

Chief Engineer of the *U.S.S. Enterprise* is Lieutenant Commander Montgomery Scott.

A proud Scot, 'Scotty' has proven himself to be the ultimate miracle worker in keeping the huge starship together for his captain.

Top left: Scotty takes the challenge with an old Claymore sword in battling the Klingons in "Day Of The Dove".

Middle left: Scotty is accused of murder in "Wolf In The Fold", while he is on shore leave with Kirk and McCoy. The case is solved when a malevolent entity that invades and controls bodies is uncovered as the real culprit.

Below: Scotty, at his best, working in a Jefferies tube in the episode "That Which Survives". The Losirians have sabotaged the ship, sending it 1,000 light years away. After some polarity changes, Scott succeeds in averting the danger and returning the ship to its correct course and heading.

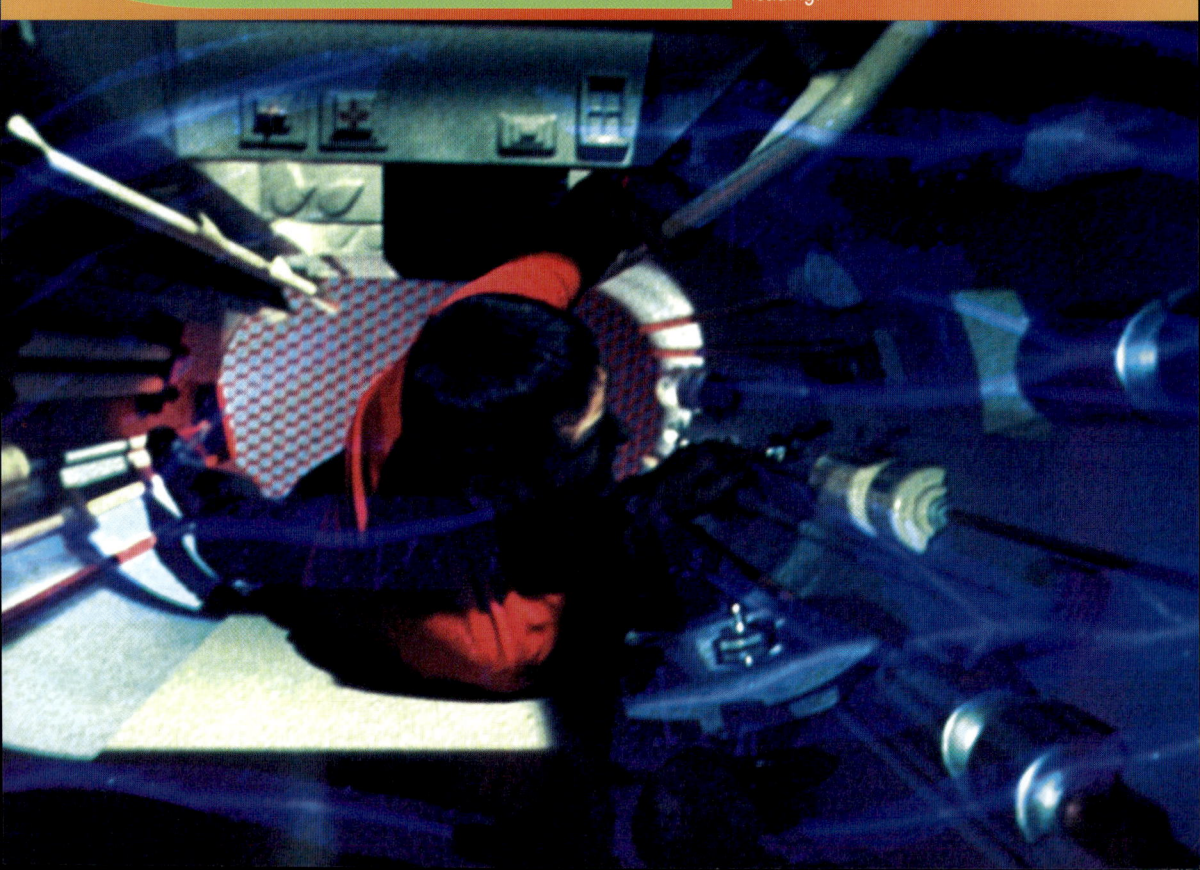

MARCH						1997		APRIL						1997		MAY						1997
M	T	W	T	F	S	S		M	T	W	T	F	S	S		M	T	W	T	F	S	S
31					1	2			1	2	3	4	5	6					1	2	3	4
3	4	5	6	7	8	9		7	8	9	10	11	12	13		5	6	7	8	9	10	11
10	11	12	13	14	15	16		14	15	16	17	18	19	20		12	13	14	15	16	17	18
17	18	19	20	21	22	23		21	22	23	24	25	26	27		19	20	21	22	23	24	25
24	25	26	27	28	29	30		28	29	30						26	27	28	29	30	31	

APRIL

MONDAY 7

Family Day (South Africa)

TUESDAY 8

WEDNESDAY 9

THURSDAY 10

FRIDAY 11

SATURDAY 12

SUNDAY 13

MEDICAL PERSPECTIVE

Top left: Dr McCoy administers to Lieutenant Uhura, who is suffering from apparent hallucinations, following the disappearance of Kirk in the episode "The Tholian Web". After Kirk is lost, the crew must come to terms with their grief. However, Uhura believes Kirk is alive after seeing the captain.

Middle left: Dr McCoy shows his skills at dealing with other cultures. In "Friday's Child", he tells the leader of the Ten Tribes that what "the Klingon has to say is unimportant" or a lie.

Below: In the episode, "The Return Of The Archons", it is Spock who plays the doctor to Dr McCoy. Dr McCoy has been "absorbed" after the crew were taken captive by a society that is totally automated. Every day at 6:00pm during "Festival", all the inhabitants become wild, brawling groups — only to return to normal the next morning.

Kirk discovers the truth and the computer known as Landru is terminated.

MARCH						1997		APRIL						1997		MAY						1997
M	T	W	T	F	S	S		M	T	W	T	F	S	S		M	T	W	T	F	S	S
31					1	2			1	2	3	4	5	6					1	2	3	4
3	4	5	6	7	8	9		7	8	9	10	11	12	13		5	6	7	8	9	10	11
10	11	12	13	14	15	16		14	15	16	17	18	19	20		12	13	14	15	16	17	18
17	18	19	20	21	22	23		21	22	23	24	25	26	27		19	20	21	22	23	24	25
24	25	26	27	28	29	30		28	29	30						26	27	28	29	30	31	

APRIL

MONDAY 14

TUESDAY 15

WEDNESDAY 16

THURSDAY 17

Avery Brooks' Birthday (Captain Sisko)

FRIDAY 18

SATURDAY 19

George Takei's Birthday (Lieutenant Sulu)

SUNDAY 20

THE DEVIL IN THE DARK

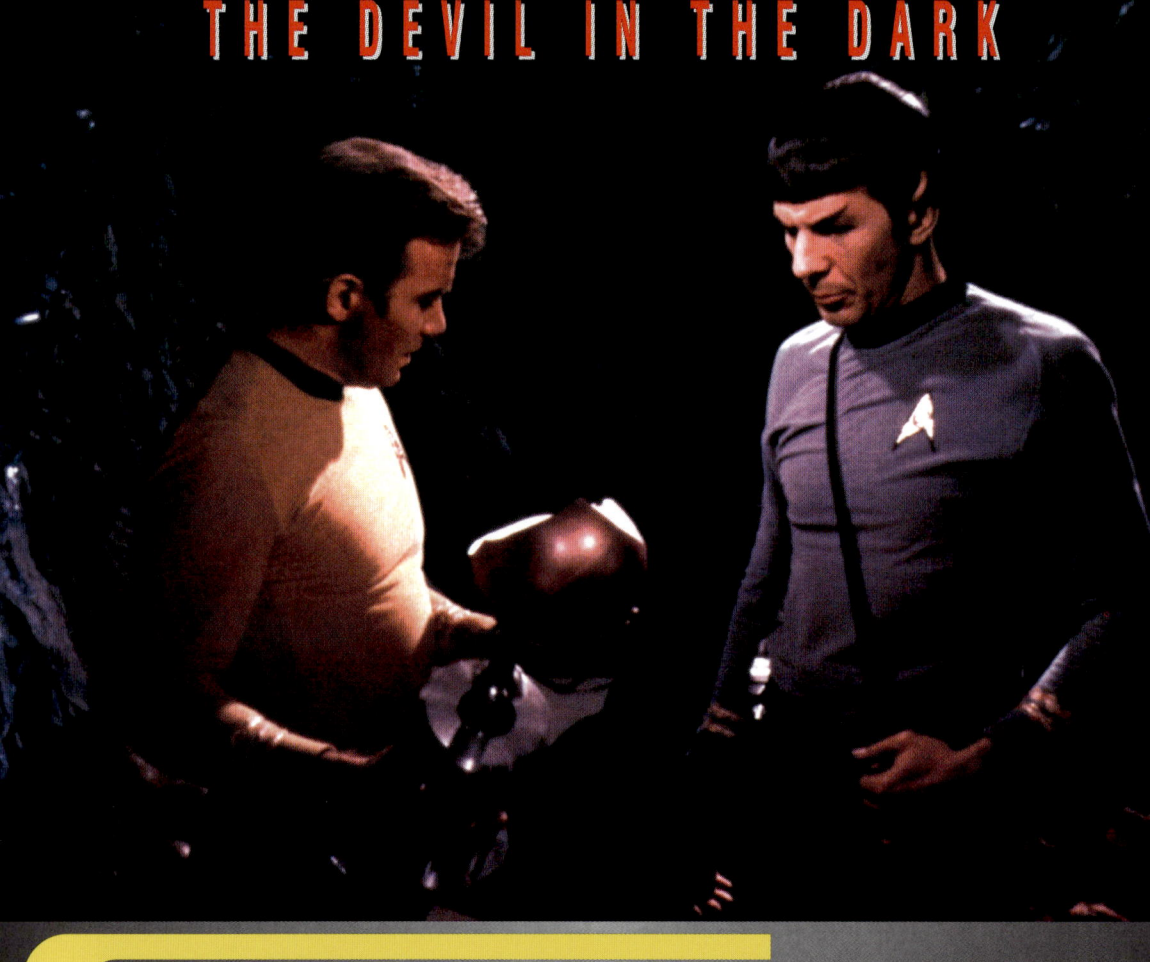

Above: In the episode, "The Devil In The Dark", Kirk and Spock discover that pergium mining operations are being sabotaged by a mother protecting her offspring. The strange rock creature, Horta, is a silicon-based life form. This episode is notable, in that William Shatner's (Kirk) father died during filming. He was helped in this sad time by the great crew, in particular, Leonard Nimoy (Mr Spock).

Below left: Mark Lenard is first seen on STAR TREK as the Romulan Commander who has a fatal run-in with Captain Kirk and the *U.S.S. Enterprise*. He is reincarnated to go on and portray Sarek (Spock's father) and a Klingon commander in STAR TREK THE MOTION PICTURE.

Below right: Kirk and Spock embark on a difficult adventure to reign in a Federation adviser, who has modelled the political system of the planet Ekos on Nazi Germany, in a bid to make the government more efficient.

MARCH						1997		APRIL						1997		MAY						1997
M	T	W	T	F	S	S		M	T	W	T	F	S	S		M	T	W	T	F	S	S
31					1	2			1	2	3	4	5	6					1	2	3	4
3	4	5	6	7	8	9		7	8	9	10	11	12	13		5	6	7	8	9	10	11
10	11	12	13	14	15	16		14	15	16	17	18	19	20		12	13	14	15	16	17	18
17	18	19	20	21	22	23		21	22	23	24	25	26	27		19	20	21	22	23	24	25
24	25	26	27	28	29	30		28	29	30						26	27	28	29	30	31	

APRIL

MONDAY 21

Passover
Earth Day (USA)

TUESDAY 22

St George's Day (UK)

WEDNESDAY 23

THURSDAY 24

Anzac Day (Australia, New Zealand)

FRIDAY 25

SATURDAY 26

Freedom Day (South Africa)

SUNDAY 27

THESE ARE THE VOYAGES OF THE *STARSHIP ENTERPRISE*

Above left: In "The Doomsday Machine", Captain Kirk faces the dilemma of re-taking the command of his ship after it is commandeered by Commodore Decker. Decker, recovering after his entire crew and ship, *U.S.S. Constellation*, was destroyed by a killing machine that was a remnant of long lost war, is distraught and full of vengeance. It is Spock following a direct order from Kirk, who finally relieves the Commodore of command.

Above right: Lieutenant Uhura has the critical post of communications officer. When travelling the farthest reaches of space, maintaining clear and accurate communications can often mean the difference between life and death. She is seen here opening a channel to Kirk in the episode "That Which Survives".

Below left: In the episode "Tomorrow Is Yesterday", Kirk and Sulu have to get the wing camera records from the Air Force files to cover the UFO sighting of the *U.S.S. Enterprise*.

Below right: Sulu becomes a swashbuckling pirate who looks to save the "fair maiden" Uhura in the episode "The Naked Time". The crew, infected by a virus picked up by a landing party crew member, is suffering from delusions.

APRIL						1997	MAY						1997	JUNE						1997
M	T	W	T	F	S	S	M	T	W	T	F	S	S	M	T	W	T	F	S	S
	1	2	3	4	5	6				1	2	3	4	30						1
7	8	9	10	11	12	13	5	6	7	8	9	10	11	2	3	4	5	6	7	8
14	15	16	17	18	19	20	12	13	14	15	16	17	18	9	10	11	12	13	14	15
21	22	23	24	25	26	27	19	20	21	22	23	24	25	16	17	18	19	20	21	22
28	29	30					26	27	28	29	30	31		23	24	25	26	27	28	29

APRIL - MAY

MONDAY 28

Kate Mulgrew's Birthday (Captain Kathryn Janeway)

Greenery Day (Japan)

TUESDAY 29

WEDNESDAY 30

Labour Day (May Day) (France, Germany)
Workers' Day (South Africa)

THURSDAY 1

FRIDAY 2

Constitutional Memorial Day (Kempo Kinen-Bi, Japan)

SATURDAY 3

SUNDAY 4

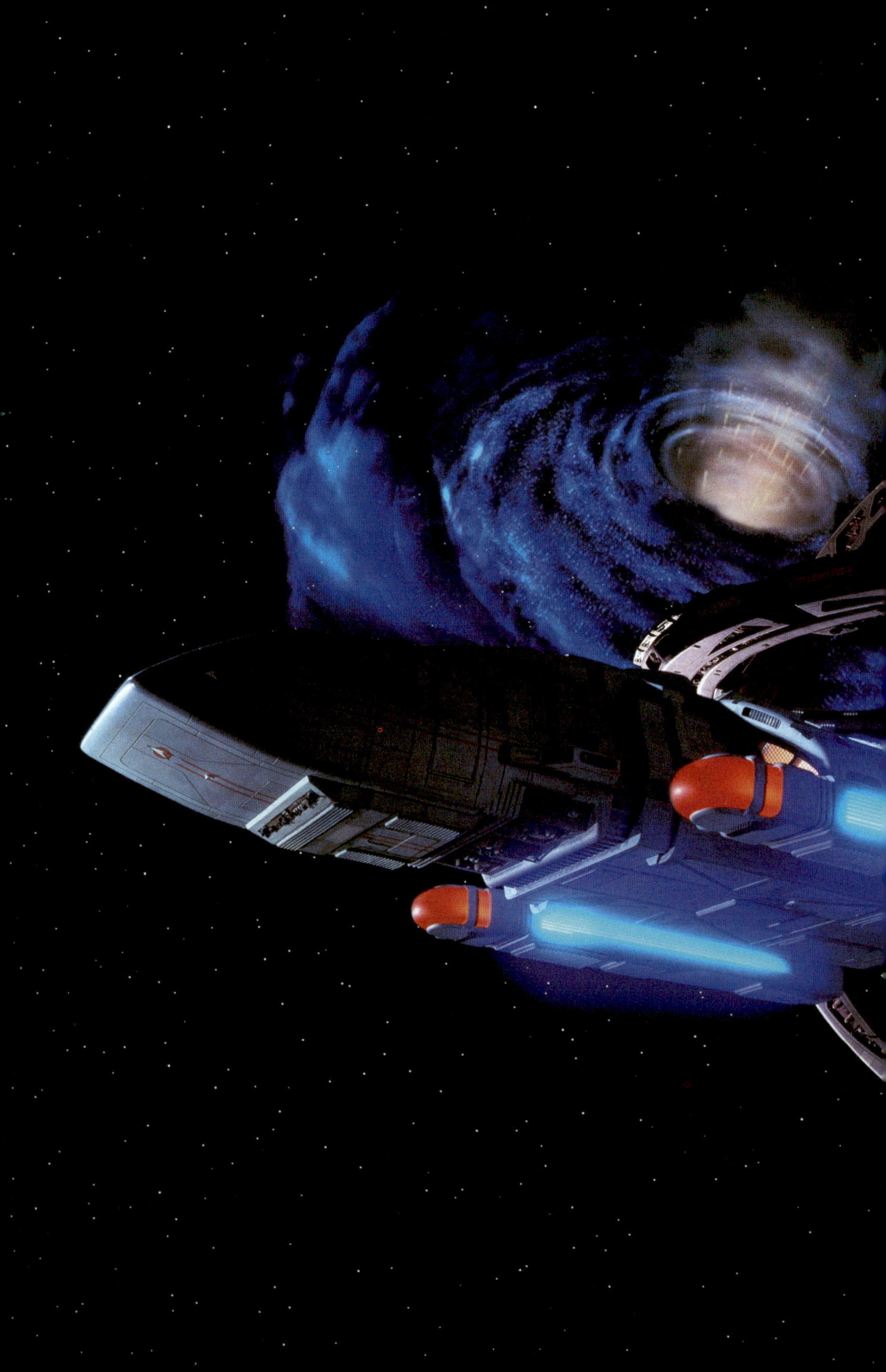

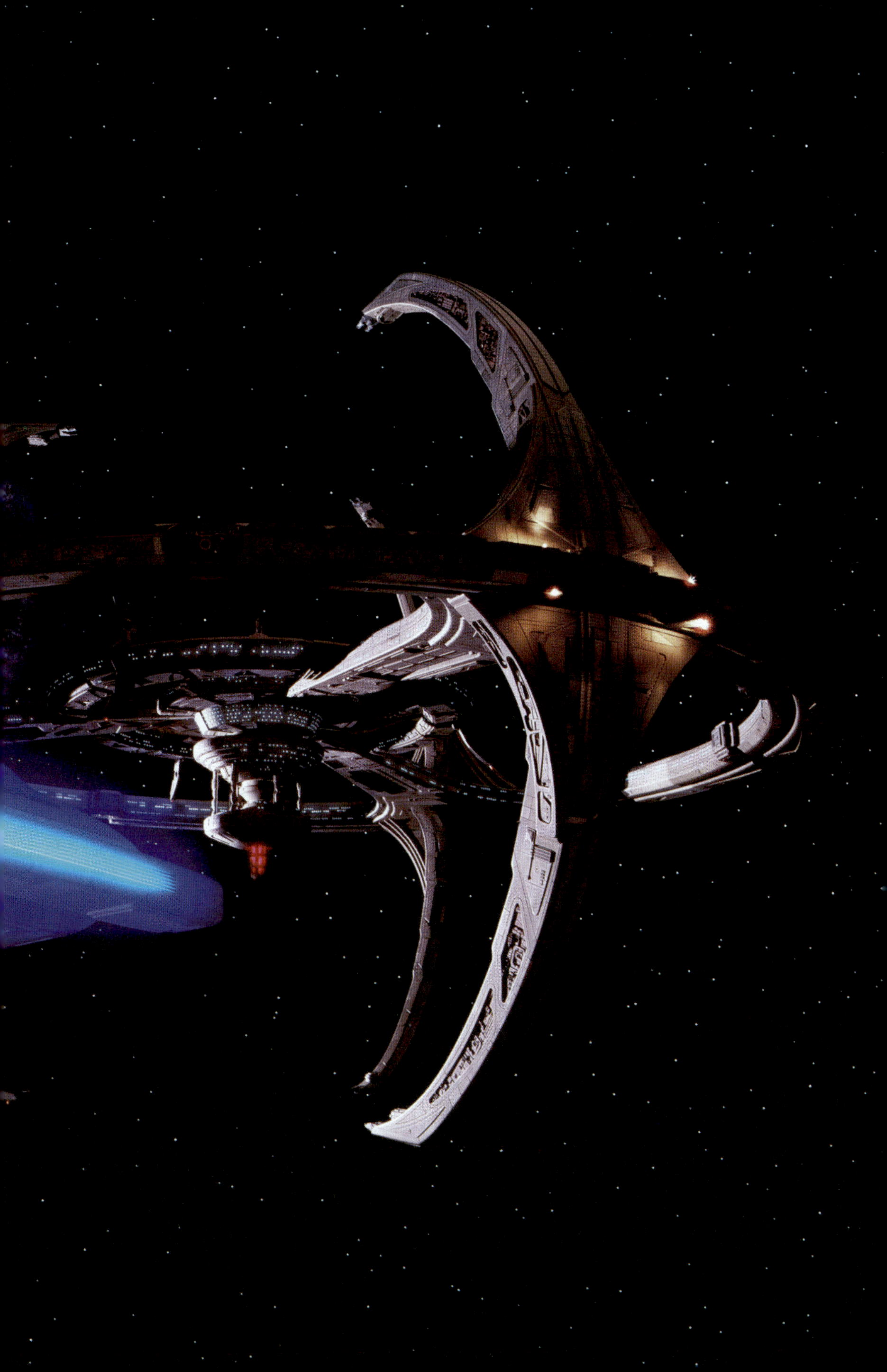

CAPTAIN BENJAMIN SISKO

Captain Sisko is the commander of Space Station *Deep Space 9*.

At the end of season three, he received his promotion to captain. Adding to his responsibilities is command of the *U.S.S. Defiant*.

With this powerful starship at his disposal, Sisko is better able to protect the station and planet Bajor against the threat of the Dominion.

APRIL					1997		MAY					1997		JUNE					1997	
M	T	W	T	F	S	S	M	T	W	T	F	S	S	M	T	W	T	F	S	S
	1	2	3	4	5	6				1	2	3	4	30						1
7	8	9	10	11	12	13	5	6	7	8	9	10	11	2	3	4	5	6	7	8
14	15	16	17	18	19	20	12	13	14	15	16	17	18	9	10	11	12	13	14	15
21	22	23	24	25	26	27	19	20	21	22	23	24	25	16	17	18	19	20	21	22
28	29	30					26	27	28	29	30	31		23	24	25	26	27	28	29

MAY

May Day Bank Holiday (UK, Ireland)

MONDAY 5

TUESDAY 6

WEDNESDAY 7

Armistice Day 1945 (France)
Ascension Day (Germany)

THURSDAY 8

FRIDAY 9

SATURDAY 10

Mother's Day (Germany, USA)

SUNDAY 11

IT'S A MATTER OF TIME

Top right: In "Through The Looking Glass", Sisko finds himself in a mirror universe where he has to mimic his mirror in order to save his late wife Jennifer.

Sisko succeeds in the mirror universe in saving Jennifer, whereas he could not save her from the Borg destruction of the fleet.

Below right: In the episode "Facets", Jadzia Dax comes to terms with her feelings of inferiority when she meets past hosts in an ancient Trill rite of closure. She and Curzon, temporarily "hosted" by Odo, meet. Dax finally finds out why Curzon said she should not be a host.

APRIL						1997		MAY						1997		JUNE						1997
M	T	W	T	F	S	S		M	T	W	T	F	S	S		M	T	W	T	F	S	S
	1	2	3	4	5	6					1	2	3	4		30						1
7	8	9	10	11	12	13		5	6	7	8	9	10	11		2	3	4	5	6	7	8
14	15	16	17	18	19	20		12	13	14	15	16	17	18		9	10	11	12	13	14	15
21	22	23	24	25	26	27		19	20	21	22	23	24	25		16	17	18	19	20	21	22
28	29	30						26	27	28	29	30	31			23	24	25	26	27	28	29

◀ MAY ▶

MONDAY 12

TUESDAY 13

WEDNESDAY 14

THURSDAY 15

FRIDAY 16

Armed Forces Day (USA)

SATURDAY 17

Ascension Day (France)
Mother's Day (Australia)

SUNDAY 18

ALIEN PRESENCE

Above: The Ferengi brothers Quark and Rom rarely see eye-to-eye. In the episode "The Bar Association", Rom tires of workplace mistreatment at the hands of his brother. Rom helps organise all of Quark's employees to form a union and goes on strike against the bar.

Right: In the episode "Return To Grace", the demoted Cardassian Gul Dukat finds he has an unexpected ally in Kira.

Kira prepares to travel to a Cardassian outpost to share Bajoran intelligence about the Klingon Empire, at the behest of First Minister Shakaar. She is surprised to discover that her old nemesis, Gul Dukat, is the commander of the freighter that will take her to the outpost.

APRIL						1997		MAY						1997		JUNE						1997
M	T	W	T	F	S	S		M	T	W	T	F	S	S		M	T	W	T	F	S	S
	1	2	3	4	5	6					1	2	3	4		30						1
7	8	9	10	11	12	13		5	6	7	8	9	10	11		2	3	4	5	6	7	8
14	15	16	17	18	19	20		12	13	14	15	16	17	18		9	10	11	12	13	14	15
21	22	23	24	25	26	27		19	20	21	22	23	24	25		16	17	18	19	20	21	22
28	29	30						26	27	28	29	30	31			23	24	25	26	27	28	29

MAY

Victoria Day (Canada)
Whitmonday (France, Germany)

MONDAY 19

TUESDAY 20

WEDNESDAY 21

THURSDAY 22

FRIDAY 23

SATURDAY 24

SUNDAY 25

THE WOMEN OF SPACE STATION DEEP SPACE 9

Left: Major Kira Nerys is *Deep Space 9*'s first officer. Coming from a background of resistance fighting against the oppressive Cardassians, she has been given the challenging role to be Bajor's advocate aboard the Station.

Right: Jadzia Dax is the science officer on board the station. Jadzia is a Trill, a symbiont species, now playing host to Dax. Captain Sisko was acquainted with Dax, when the host body was Curzon, a much older man. Yet Sisko and Jadzia have a close friendship, the captain affectionately calling her "old man". But this Dax host is an extremely talented scientist, a change from the rogue that was the prior host.

MAY						1997		JUNE						1997		JULY						1997
M	T	W	T	F	S	S		M	T	W	T	F	S	S		M	T	W	T	F	S	S
			1	2	3	4		30						1			1	2	3	4	5	6
5	6	7	8	9	10	11		2	3	4	5	6	7	8		7	8	9	10	11	12	13
12	13	14	15	16	17	18		9	10	11	12	13	14	15		14	15	16	17	18	19	20
19	20	21	22	23	24	25		16	17	18	19	20	21	22		21	22	23	24	25	26	27
26	27	28	29	30	31			23	24	25	26	27	28	29		28	29	30	31			

MAY - JUNE

Memorial Day (Observed, USA)
Spring Holiday (UK)

MONDAY 26

TUESDAY 27

WEDNESDAY 28

Corpus Christi Day (Germany)

THURSDAY 29

Michael Piller's Birthday (Executive Producer, ST: TNG; Co-Creator, Executive Producer, ST: DS9, ST: VGR)

Colm Meaney's Birthday (Chief O'Brien)

Memorial Day (USA)

FRIDAY 30

SATURDAY 31

René Auberjonois' Birthday (Constable Odo)

SUNDAY 1

THE NAME IS BASHIR... JULIAN BASHIR

Right: Dr Bashir is enjoying a holosuite program that casts him as a super suave, 1960s Earth secret agent. Suddenly, Garak intrudes on his fantasy, convincing the doctor to let him stay.

At the same time, Sisko, Kira, Dax, Worf, and O'Brien transport from a runabout just before sabotage causes it to explode. The force blows out the transporter during the beam-out rescue attempt. The only place that has enough memory to store their patterns is the holosuite.

Above left: Kira is now Anastasia, a Russian spy and sometime ally of the "spy" Bashir. Bashir must let the program play out if there is any hope of saving his crew mates.

Above right: The normal unassuming doctor when he is not holodeck programming.

MAY						1997		JUNE						1997		JULY						1997
M	T	W	T	F	S	S		M	T	W	T	F	S	S		M	T	W	T	F	S	S
			1	2	3	4		30						1			1	2	3	4	5	6
5	6	7	8	9	10	11		2	3	4	5	6	7	8		7	8	9	10	11	12	13
12	13	14	15	16	17	18		9	10	11	12	13	14	15		14	15	16	17	18	19	20
19	20	21	22	23	24	25		16	17	18	19	20	21	22		21	22	23	24	25	26	27
26	27	28	29	30	31			23	24	25	26	27	28	29		28	29	30	31			

JUNE

Bank Holiday (Ireland)
Queen's Birthday (New Zealand)

MONDAY 2

TUESDAY 3

WEDNESDAY 4

THURSDAY 5

Jeri Taylor's Birthday (Executive Producer, ST: TNG, ST: VGR; Co-Creator ST: VGR)

FRIDAY 6

SATURDAY 7

SUNDAY 8

NEVER A DULL MOMENT

Above: Kira and Dax, just out from the holosuite, are introduced to Lieutenant Commander Worf by Chief O'Brien. Worf was assigned to *Deep Space 9* to assist in negotiations with the Klingons.

Left: In the episode "Indiscretion", a Bajoran smuggler tells Major Kira he has recovered a piece of metal that might be from the *Ravinok*, a Cardassian ship that disappeared six years ago with a group of Bajoran prisoners.

A good friend of Kira's was among those lost, and she makes immediate plans to investigate, but learns a Cardassian representative wants to accompany her. Kira reluctantly agrees, then discovers that the representative is Gul Dukat.

On the planet, Kira discovers thast Dukat was in love with a Bajoran woman who died in the crash. But his daughter by her may have survived.

MAY						1997		JUNE						1997		JULY						1997
M	T	W	T	F	S	S		M	T	W	T	F	S	S		M	T	W	T	F	S	S
			1	2	3	4		30						1			1	2	3	4	5	6
5	6	7	8	9	10	11		2	3	4	5	6	7	8		7	8	9	10	11	12	13
12	13	14	15	16	17	18		9	10	11	12	13	14	15		14	15	16	17	18	19	20
19	20	21	22	23	24	25		16	17	18	19	20	21	22		21	22	23	24	25	26	27
26	27	28	29	30	31			23	24	25	26	27	28	29		28	29	30	31			

JUNE

Queen's Birthday Holiday (Australia, except WA)

MONDAY 9

TUESDAY 10

WEDNESDAY 11

THURSDAY 12

FRIDAY 13

Flag Day (USA)

SATURDAY 14

Father's Day (UK, USA)

SUNDAY 15

CHIEF MILES O'BRIEN

Chief O'Brien is the technical mastermind of the basic operation of the space station.

After a successful tour of duty on the *U.S.S. Enterprise NCC-1701-D*, under the command of Captain Jean-Luc Picard, O'Brien opted for the challenge of a remote space station.

Saddled with a stripped Cardassian outpost station, instead of state-of-the-art Federation technology, he has to keep the station operational by creatively maintaining the already abused circuitry.

Couple this with having a wife and child to care for, he truly has his hands full.

MAY						1997		JUNE						1997		JULY						1997
M	T	W	T	F	S	S		M	T	W	T	F	S	S		M	T	W	T	F	S	S
			1	2	3	4		30						1			1	2	3	4	5	6
5	6	7	8	9	10	11		2	3	4	5	6	7	8		7	8	9	10	11	12	13
12	13	14	15	16	17	18		9	10	11	12	13	14	15		14	15	16	17	18	19	20
19	20	21	22	23	24	25		16	17	18	19	20	21	22		21	22	23	24	25	26	27
26	27	28	29	30	31			23	24	25	26	27	28	29		28	29	30	31			

JUNE

Youth Day (South Africa)   **MONDAY 16**

TUESDAY 17

WEDNESDAY 18

THURSDAY 19

FRIDAY 20

SATURDAY 21

Tim Russ's Birthday (Tactical and Security Officer Lt. Tuvok)

SUNDAY 22

KLINGON KAPERS

Above: In the episode, "The Sword Of Kahless", Worf and Dax assist Kor, a revered Klingon warrior, to search for a mythical, ancient artifact. They believe it has the power to unite the Klingon Empire.

Right: In the episode "The Sons Of Mogh", Worf's brother Kurn arrives unexpectedly and asks Worf to kill him. He explains that since Worf sided with the Federation against the Klingon Empire, Kurn and his family are outcasts on Homeworld.

Worf makes the ultimate sacrifice and has Kurn's features altered and memory erased, allowing him to regain his place in Klingon society.

Unfortunately, Worf has now lost not only his last link to the Klingon society forever, but his brother as well.

MAY						1997	JUNE						1997	JULY						1997
M	T	W	T	F	S	S	M	T	W	T	F	S	S	M	T	W	T	F	S	S
			1	2	3	4	30						1		1	2	3	4	5	6
5	6	7	8	9	10	11	2	3	4	5	6	7	8	7	8	9	10	11	12	13
12	13	14	15	16	17	18	9	10	11	12	13	14	15	14	15	16	17	18	19	20
19	20	21	22	23	24	25	16	17	18	19	20	21	22	21	22	23	24	25	26	27
26	27	28	29	30	31		23	24	25	26	27	28	29	28	29	30	31			

JUNE

MONDAY 23

TUESDAY 24

WEDNESDAY 25

THURSDAY 26

FRIDAY 27

SATURDAY 28

SUNDAY **29**

LIEUTENANT COMMANDER WORF

Season four of STAR TREK: DEE
SPACE NINE introduces Lieutenar
Commander Worf to the station.

Assigned to discover what th
Klingon Empire is planning to do, Wo
turns on his own people and help
Starfleet. Worf is persuaded to stay o
as Strategic Officer.

Though still not comfortable, h
begins to adjust to a new assignmer
aboard Space Station *Deep Space 9*.

JUNE						1997		JULY						1997		AUGUST						1997
M	T	W	T	F	S	S		M	T	W	T	F	S	S		M	T	W	T	F	S	S
30						1			1	2	3	4	5	6							1	2	3
2	3	4	5	6	7	8		7	8	9	10	11	12	13		4	5	6	7	8	9	10
9	10	11	12	13	14	15		14	15	16	17	18	19	20		11	12	13	14	15	16	17
16	17	18	19	20	21	22		21	22	23	24	25	26	27		18	19	20	21	22	23	24
23	24	25	26	27	28	29		28	29	30	31					25	26	27	28	29	30	31

JUNE-JULY

MONDAY 30

Canada Day (Canada)

TUESDAY 1

WEDNESDAY 2

THURSDAY 3

Independence Day (USA)

FRIDAY 4

SATURDAY 5

SUNDAY 6

U.S.S. VOYAGER NCC-74656

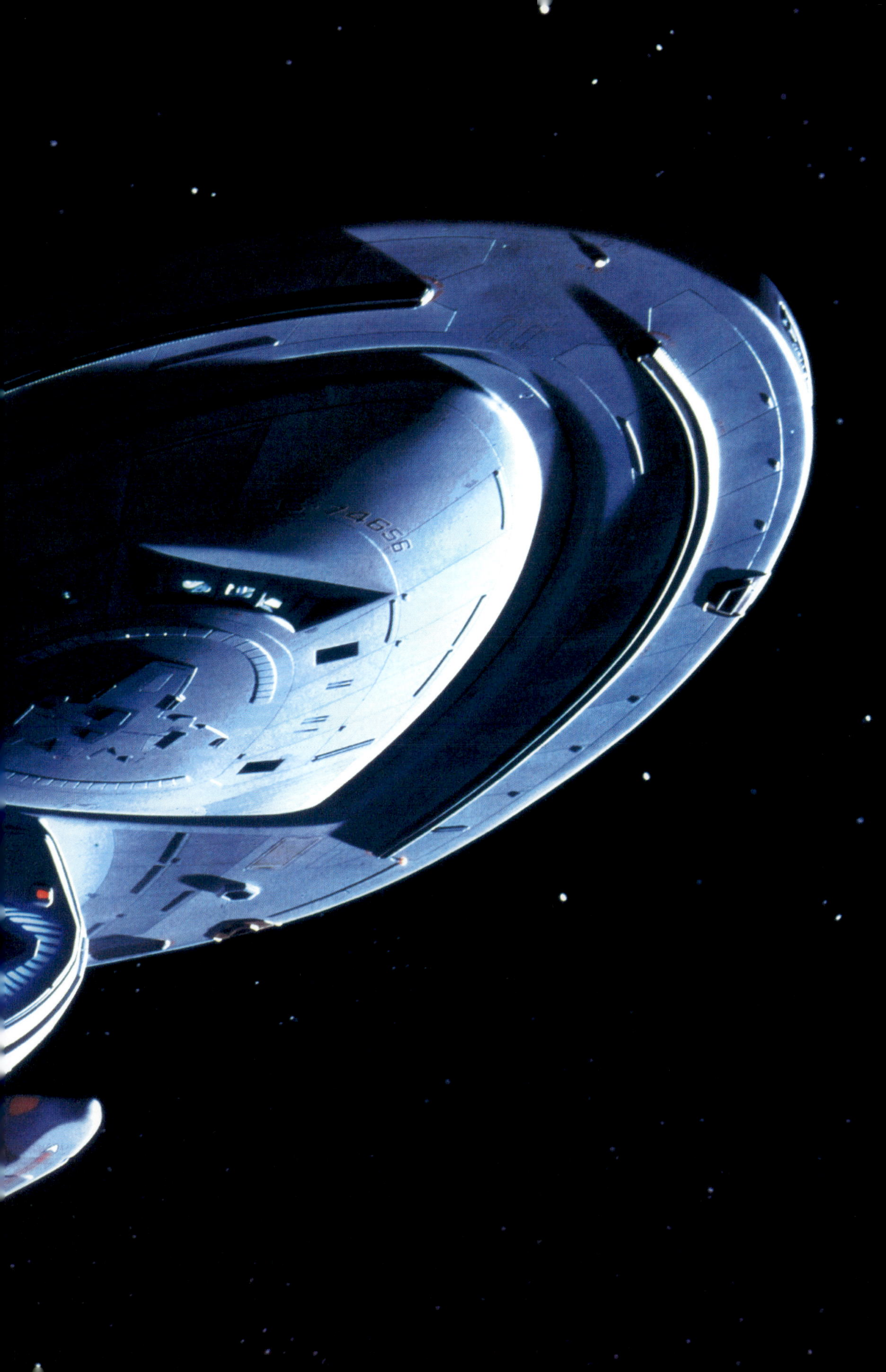
74656

CAPTAIN KATHRYN JANEWAY

Captain of the *U.S.S. Voyager* is Kathryn Janeway, who must lead her hybrid crew on the long journey back to Federation space.

Flung many thousands of light years away to the Delta Quadrant, Janeway has to co-ordinate a crew comprising the remnants of her original manifest and those of the rebel Maquis whose own ship was destroyed.

The journey home will test her mettle as captain.

JUNE						1997	JULY						1997	AUGUST						1997
M	T	W	T	F	S	S	M	T	W	T	F	S	S	M	T	W	T	F	S	S
30						1		1	2	3	4	5	6					1	2	3
2	3	4	5	6	7	8	7	8	9	10	11	12	13	4	5	6	7	8	9	10
9	10	11	12	13	14	15	14	15	16	17	18	19	20	11	12	13	14	15	16	17
16	17	18	19	20	21	22	21	22	23	24	25	26	27	18	19	20	21	22	23	24
23	24	25	26	27	28	29	28	29	30	31				25	26	27	28	29	30	31

JULY

MONDAY **7**

TUESDAY **8**

WEDNESDAY **9**

THURSDAY **10**

FRIDAY **11**

SATURDAY **12**

Holiday (Northern Ireland)
Patrick Stewart's Birthday (Captain Jean-Luc Picard)

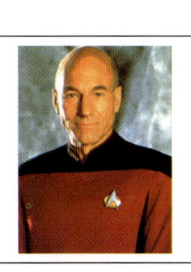

SUNDAY **13**

THE ADVENTURE BEGINS – AGAIN

Above: In "Death Wish", a rebel Q escapes imprisonment from inside a comet and demands asylum aboard the *U.S.S. Voyager*. He tries to explain to Captain Janeway that the boredom of omnipotence can have only one escape – death.

Below: In the episode "Dreadnought" (directed by LeVar Burton), the *Starship Voyager* spots a Cardassian-designed, self-guided missile carrying a warhead capable of significant destructive force. It is imperative to disarm the weapon, as it is on a course for the heavily populated planet Rakosa.

JUNE						1997		JULY						1997		AUGUST						1997
M	T	W	T	F	S	S		M	T	W	T	F	S	S		M	T	W	T	F	S	S
30						1			1	2	3	4	5	6						1	2	3
2	3	4	5	6	7	8		7	8	9	10	11	12	13		4	5	6	7	8	9	10
9	10	11	12	13	14	15		14	15	16	17	18	19	20		11	12	13	14	15	16	17
16	17	18	19	20	21	22		21	22	23	24	25	26	27		18	19	20	21	22	23	24
23	24	25	26	27	28	29		28	29	30	31					25	26	27	28	29	30	31

JULY

Bastille Day (France)

MONDAY 14

TUESDAY 15

WEDNESDAY 16

THURSDAY 17

FRIDAY 18

SATURDAY 19

SUNDAY 20

CAPTAIN JANEWAY TO THE RESCUE

Right: In the episode "Resistance", Janeway, Tuvok, Torres and Neelix transport to an Alsaurian city in search of precious tellerium needed to power the ship. The city is occupied by the hostile Mokra soldiers, who are tipped off to the *U.S.S. Voyager*'s presence and capture Tuvok and Torres. During the commotion, Janeway is secreted away by Caylem, a local eccentric who believes the captain is his long lost daughter.

Below: Commander William T. Riker returns courtesy of his old "friend" Q, in the episode "Death Wish". Riker is called as a witness in an asylum hearing. He tells how a member of the Q Continuum saved an ancestor.

JUNE						1997	JULY						1997	AUGUST						1997
M	T	W	T	F	S	S	M	T	W	T	F	S	S	M	T	W	T	F	S	S
30						1		1	2	3	4	5	6					1	2	3
2	3	4	5	6	7	8	7	8	9	10	11	12	13	4	5	6	7	8	9	10
9	10	11	12	13	14	15	14	15	16	17	18	19	20	11	12	13	14	15	16	17
16	17	18	19	20	21	22	21	22	23	24	25	26	27	18	19	20	21	22	23	24
23	24	25	26	27	28	29	28	29	30	31				25	26	27	28	29	30	31

JULY

MONDAY 21

TUESDAY 22

WEDNESDAY 23

THURSDAY 24

FRIDAY 25

Nana Visitor's Birthday (Major Kira Nerys)

SATURDAY 26

SUNDAY 27

CHIEF ENGINEER B'ELANNA TORRES

In the episode "Prototype", the crew finds floating in space a deactivated humanoid robot with an unfamiliar power source. Chief Engineer B'Elanna Torres is able to repair this mysterious mechanical "man". When it comes to "life", the sentient artificial lifeform, Automated Unit 3947, explains that its kind is near extinction and asks Chief Engineer Torres to build a prototype for construction of more units.

In accordance with the Prime Directive, Torres declines the request. However, when 3947's Pralor homeship is located, the robot abducts her and threatens to destroy the *U.S.S. Voyager* unless she constructs the prototype.

JULY						1997		AUGUST						1997		SEPTEMBER						1997
M	T	W	T	F	S	S		M	T	W	T	F	S	S		M	T	W	T	F	S	S
	1	2	3	4	5	6						1	2	3		1	2	3	4	5	6	7
7	8	9	10	11	12	13		4	5	6	7	8	9	10		8	9	10	11	12	13	14
14	15	16	17	18	19	20		11	12	13	14	15	16	17		15	16	17	18	19	20	21
21	22	23	24	25	26	27		18	19	20	21	22	23	24		22	23	24	25	26	27	28
28	29	30	31					25	26	27	28	29	30	31		29	30					

JULY-AUGUST

MONDAY 28

Wil Wheaton's Birthday (Ensign Wesley Crusher)

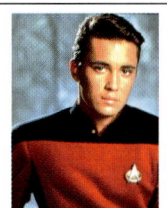

TUESDAY 29

WEDNESDAY 30

THURSDAY 31

FRIDAY 1

SATURDAY 2

SUNDAY 3

NEW ADVENTURES

Above: A confused Ensign Harry Kim in the episode "Non Sequitur", awakens to find himself on Earth. He is working as a design specialist at Starfleet Engineering and engaged to be married to his sweetheart Libby, instead of serving on the *Starship Voyager*.

Below left: The holographic doctor is always looking at ways to improve his bedside manner.

Below right: The crew is hailed by Ocampa colonists on an alien space station in the episode, "Cold Fire". They are led to the female mate of the Caretaker, a mysterious being who has the ability to send them home. As Tuvok tutors Kes in honing her rapidly maturing mental abilities, it's concluded that her burgeoning powers have been extremely underestimated.

JULY						1997		AUGUST						1997		SEPTEMBER						1997
M	T	W	T	F	S	S		M	T	W	T	F	S	S		M	T	W	T	F	S	S
	1	2	3	4	5	6						1	2	3		1	2	3	4	5	6	7
7	8	9	10	11	12	13		4	5	6	7	8	9	10		8	9	10	11	12	13	14
14	15	16	17	18	19	20		11	12	13	14	15	16	17		15	16	17	18	19	20	21
21	22	23	24	25	26	27		18	19	20	21	22	23	24		22	23	24	25	26	27	28
28	29	30	31					25	26	27	28	29	30	31		29	30					

AUGUST

Bank Holiday (Republic of Ireland, Scotland) — **MONDAY 4**

TUESDAY 5

WEDNESDAY 6

Cirroc Lofton's Birthday (Jake Sisko)

THURSDAY 7

FRIDAY 8

SATURDAY 9

National Women's Day (South Africa) — **SUNDAY 10**

LIEUTENANT TUVOK

Lieutenant Tuvok is the starfleet tactical and security officer aboard the *U.S.S. Voyager*. He enjoys a close working relationship with Captain Janeway, and uses his powerful combination of wisdom, experience and physical skills to make him a valued member of the starship crew.

Above: Lieutenant Tuvok uses his Vulcan powers of mind melding to assist Kes in understanding her own telepathic powers.

Below: Tuvok confers with Neelix in the episode "Tattoo". They are part of an away team, looking for minerals on a moon's surface.

JULY						1997		AUGUST						1997		SEPTEMBER						1997
M	T	W	T	F	S	S		M	T	W	T	F	S	S		M	T	W	T	F	S	S
	1	2	3	4	5	6						1	2	3		1	2	3	4	5	6	7
7	8	9	10	11	12	13		4	5	6	7	8	9	10		8	9	10	11	12	13	14
14	15	16	17	18	19	20		11	12	13	14	15	16	17		15	16	17	18	19	20	21
21	22	23	24	25	26	27		18	19	20	21	22	23	24		22	23	24	25	26	27	28
28	29	30	31					25	26	27	28	29	30	31		29	30					

AUGUST

MONDAY 11

TUESDAY 12

WEDNESDAY 13

THURSDAY 14

Assumption Day (France, Germany)

FRIDAY 15

SATURDAY 16

SUNDAY 17

FIRST OFFICER CHAKOTAY

Above: Kazon intruders board the *U.S.S. Voyager* and steal a Transporter control module, in the episode "Maneuvers". This collateral enables their leader Culluh, to try to persuade rival sects to join together to conquer the Federation starship.

Surprisingly, the mastermind behind the Kazon's scheme is an adviser with Cardassian, Maquis and Starfleet tactical experience – none other than Seska. The despised traitor was a former intimate of Chakotay's.

Right: In the episode "Initiations", First Officer Chakotay borrows a shuttlecraft to perform the Pakra, a solitary Indian ritual commemorating his father's death. Chakotay inadvertently drifts into Kazon-Ogla territory and becomes the target of a Kazon youth attempting to earn his Ogla warrior name by killing the Federation enemy.

JULY						1997	AUGUST						1997	SEPTEMBER						1997
M	T	W	T	F	S	S	M	T	W	T	F	S	S	M	T	W	T	F	S	S
	1	2	3	4	5	6					1	2	3	1	2	3	4	5	6	7
7	8	9	10	11	12	13	4	5	6	7	8	9	10	8	9	10	11	12	13	14
14	15	16	17	18	19	20	11	12	13	14	15	16	17	15	16	17	18	19	20	21
21	22	23	24	25	26	27	18	19	20	21	22	23	24	22	23	24	25	26	27	28
28	29	30	31				25	26	27	28	29	30	31	29	30					

AUGUST

MONDAY 18

Gene Roddenberry's Birthday (STAR TREK and STAR TREK: THE NEXT GENERATION Creator and Executive Producer)

Jonathan Frakes' Birthday (Commander William T. Riker)

TUESDAY 19

WEDNESDAY 20

THURSDAY 21

FRIDAY 22

SATURDAY 23

Jennifer Lien's Birthday (Kes)

SUNDAY 24

THE VOYAGE BACK

Above: The Doctor receives information that the U.S.S. Voyager has suffered a massive attack and that most of the crew has abandoned ship in the episode "Projections". Using a remote holoprojection system, he ventures from sick bay to aid those still on board.

Exploring the near-deserted ship, the Doctor must determine what is and is not reality. Strangely, he exhibits human life signs, experiencing pain and injury.

He then meets Lieutenant Barclay, and learns of Dr Lewis Zimmerman, the holo-engineer who wrote the Doctor's medical holographic program.

Right: In the episode "Parturition", Kes spends some free time with a smitten Tom Paris. This causes Neelix to be overcome by jealousy and he instigates a messy fight with the lieutenant. Captain Janeway sends the sparring pair on a shuttle mission to a planet to replenish food supplies, after being assured that they can work together.

AUGUST						1997		SEPTEMBER					1997		OCTOBER					1997
M	T	W	T	F	S	S	M	T	W	T	F	S	S	M	T	W	T	F	S	S
				1	2	3	1	2	3	4	5	6	7			1	2	3	4	5
4	5	6	7	8	9	10	8	9	10	11	12	13	14	6	7	8	9	10	11	12
11	12	13	14	15	16	17	15	16	17	18	19	20	21	13	14	15	16	17	18	19
18	19	20	21	22	23	24	22	23	24	25	26	27	28	20	21	22	23	24	25	26
25	26	27	28	29	30	31	29	30						27	28	29	30	31		

AUGUST

Late Summer Holiday (UK) — **MONDAY 25**

TUESDAY 26

WEDNESDAY 27

Gates McFadden's Birthday (Dr Beverly Crusher) — **THURSDAY 28**

FRIDAY 29

SATURDAY 30

SUNDAY 31

NEW FRONTIERS

Above: Chakotay and Tuvok discover Amelia Earhart, the first Aviatrix on Earth in the episode "The 37's". In 1937 she was lost during a flight and never recovered. This particular episode, though filmed at the end of season one, was held over by United Paramount Network (UPN) to become the season two premiere. This story is famous as it involves Condition Blue – where the *U.S.S. Voyager* actually lands on a planet.

Below: In the episode "Initiations", Chakotay has his hands full after he rescues a Kazon boy who is intent on earning his right to be called a warrior. Despite saving the boy, Chakotay is told he now has to kill him because Chakotay has interfered in the ritual.

AUGUST						1997		SEPTEMBER						1997		OCTOBER						1997
M	T	W	T	F	S	S		M	T	W	T	F	S	S		M	T	W	T	F	S	S
				1	2	3		1	2	3	4	5	6	7				1	2	3	4	5
4	5	6	7	8	9	10		8	9	10	11	12	13	14		6	7	8	9	10	11	12
11	12	13	14	15	16	17		15	16	17	18	19	20	21		13	14	15	16	17	18	19
18	19	20	21	22	23	24		22	23	24	25	26	27	28		20	21	22	23	24	25	26
25	26	27	28	29	30	31		29	30							27	28	29	30	31		

SEPTEMBER

Labor Day (USA, Canada)

MONDAY 1

TUESDAY 2

WEDNESDAY 3

THURSDAY 4

FRIDAY 5

SATURDAY 6

Father's Day (Australia)

SUNDAY 7

MEDICAL TEAM

The Chief Medical Officer aboard the *U.S.S. Voyager* was killed when the ship was flung into the Delta Quadrant. The only known medical back up was the Emergency Medical Holographic Program – a computer composite of the experiences and knowledge of some 46 medical officers.

Captain Janeway now relies on and trusts the holographic doctor as the CMO.

Kes, an Ocampa native, picked up on the *Starship Voyager*'s first mission in the Delta Quadrant, has quickly become an invaluable medical assistant and close friend to The Doctor.

Together, they become important members of the crew, as the journey back to Alpha Quadrant is undertaken.

AUGUST						1997		SEPTEMBER						1997		OCTOBER						1997
M	T	W	T	F	S	S		M	T	W	T	F	S	S		M	T	W	T	F	S	S
				1	2	3		1	2	3	4	5	6	7				1	2	3	4	5
4	5	6	7	8	9	10		8	9	10	11	12	13	14		6	7	8	9	10	11	12
11	12	13	14	15	16	17		15	16	17	18	19	20	21		13	14	15	16	17	18	19
18	19	20	21	22	23	24		22	23	24	25	26	27	28		20	21	22	23	24	25	26
25	26	27	28	29	30	31		29	30							27	28	29	30	31		

SEPTEMBER

MONDAY 8

TUESDAY 9

WEDNESDAY 10

Roxann Biggs-Dawson's Birthday (Chief Engineer B'Elanna Torres)

THURSDAY 11

FRIDAY 12

SATURDAY 13

Walter Koenig's Birthday (Commander Pavel Chekov)

SUNDAY 14

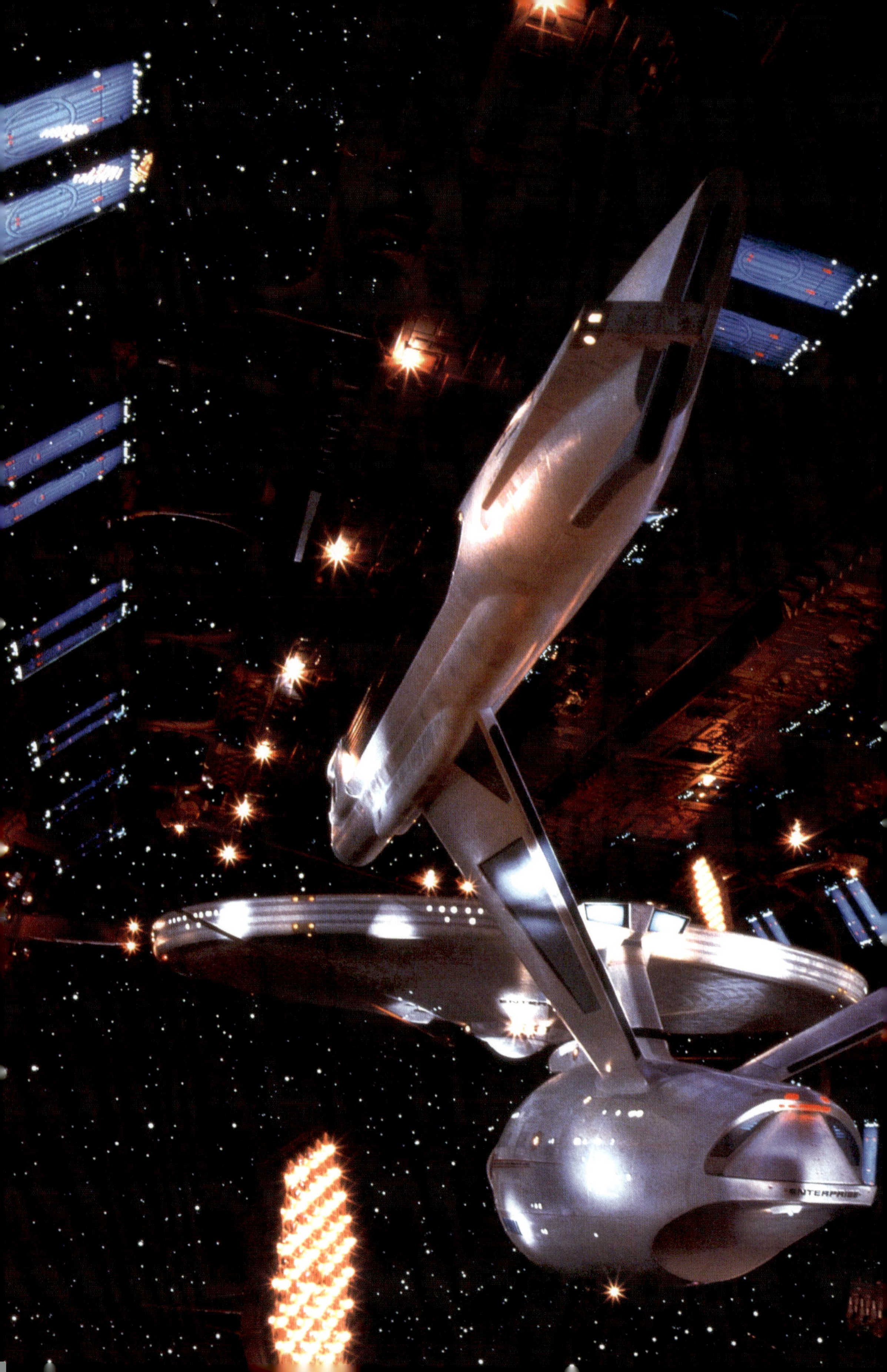
ENTERPRISE

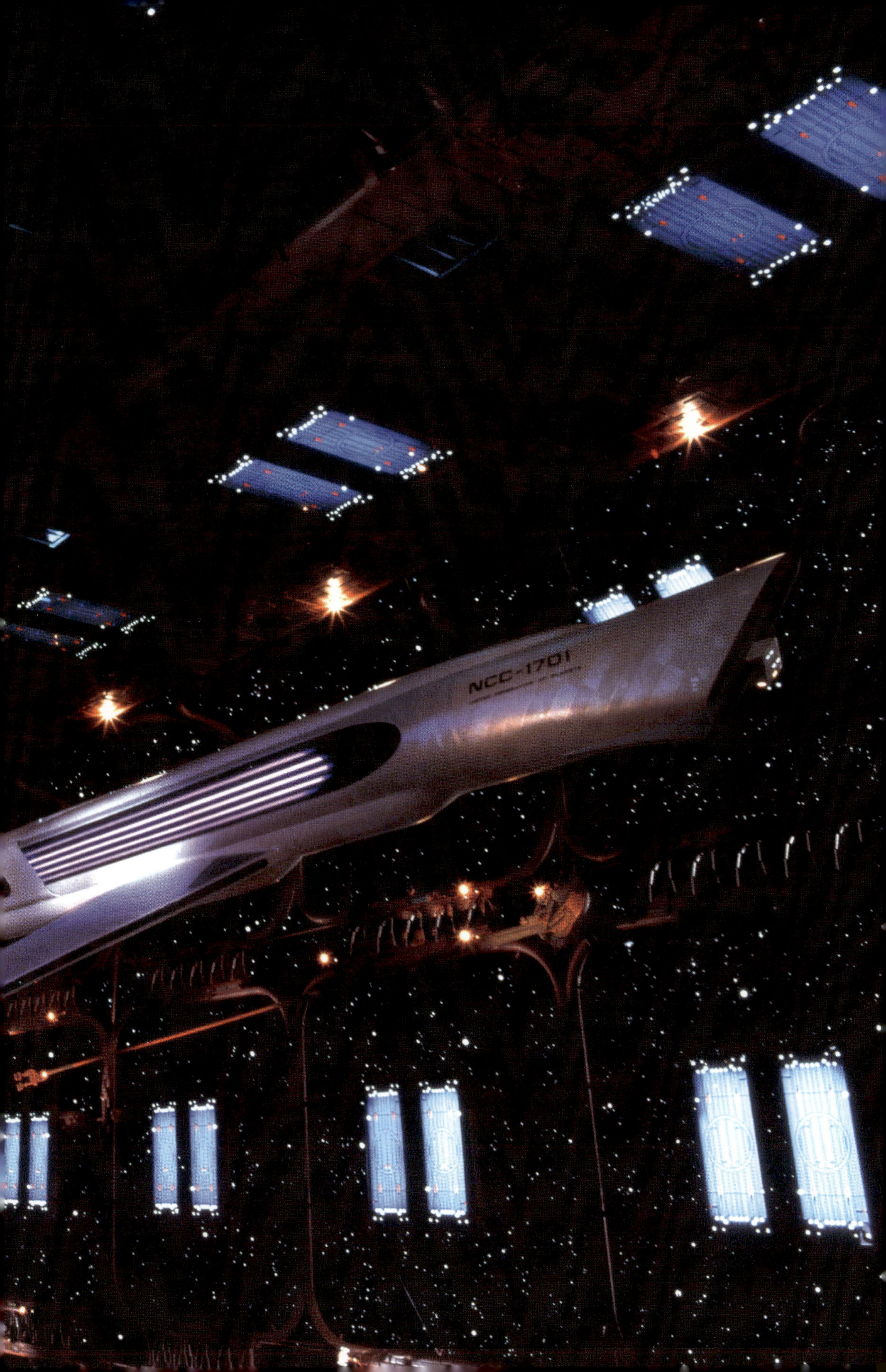
NCC-1701

STAR TREK THE MOTION PICTURE

Above: In STAR TREK THE MOTION PICTURE (1979), three Klingon cruisers come face-to-face with the huge mechanical device that calls itself V'Ger. After a brief struggle, the three ships are absorbed by the behemoth "ship".

Mark Lenard, better known for his portrayal of Spock's father "Sarek" in the original series, plays one of the doomed Klingon commanders. This completed a three-way alien score for him, having been a Romulan commander, Sarek of Vulcan and a Klingon commander.

Below: Since Spock is unavailable, on Vulcan undertaking the Kolinahr discipline, Admiral Kirk's second choice for science officer is Commander Sonak. Unfortunately, Commander Sonak and a female crew member die horribly in a transporter accident while beaming aboard the *U.S.S. Enterprise*.

AUGUST						1997		SEPTEMBER					1997		OCTOBER					1997
M	T	W	T	F	S	S	M	T	W	T	F	S	S	M	T	W	T	F	S	S
				1	2	3	1	2	3	4	5	6	7			1	2	3	4	5
4	5	6	7	8	9	10	8	9	10	11	12	13	14	6	7	8	9	10	11	12
11	12	13	14	15	16	17	15	16	17	18	19	20	21	13	14	15	16	17	18	19
18	19	20	21	22	23	24	22	23	24	25	26	27	28	20	21	22	23	24	25	26
25	26	27	28	29	30	31	29	30						27	28	29	30	31		

SEPTEMBER

Respect-For-The-Aged Day (Keiro-No-Hi, Japan)

MONDAY 15

TUESDAY 16

WEDNESDAY 17

THURSDAY 18

FRIDAY 19

SATURDAY 20

SUNDAY 21

STAR TREK III: THE SEARCH FOR SPOCK

Above: Under Admiral Kirk's command, Engineer Scott helps commandeer the *U.S.S. Enterprise* out of Spacedock. In order to prevent Captain Styles of the *U.S.S. Excelsior* from pursuing, Scott has sabotaged the transwarp drive. He is seen here handing Dr McCoy the missing components from the *U.S.S. Excelsior*.

Below: On the Genesis planet, Commander Kruge orders one of his Klingon crew to kill a hostage to show Admiral Kirk his intent. The Klingon crew member arbitrarily selects Lieutenant Saavik, but the heroic David Marcus (Kirk and Dr Carol Marcus's son) jumps to her rescue. He dies very bravely, leaving a devastated, grieving Kirk with a deep hatred for Klingons.

SEPTEMBER						1997		OCTOBER						1997		NOVEMBER						1997
M	T	W	T	F	S	S		M	T	W	T	F	S	S		M	T	W	T	F	S	S
1	2	3	4	5	6	7				1	2	3	4	5							1	2
8	9	10	11	12	13	14		6	7	8	9	10	11	12		3	4	5	6	7	8	9
15	16	17	18	19	20	21		13	14	15	16	17	18	19		10	11	12	13	14	15	16
22	23	24	25	26	27	28		20	21	22	23	24	25	26		17	18	19	20	21	22	23
29	30							27	28	29	30	31				24	25	26	27	28	29	30

SEPTEMBER-OCTOBER

MONDAY 29

Queen's Birthday (Western Australia)

TUESDAY 30

WEDNESDAY 1

THURSDAY 2

Rosh Hashanah

FRIDAY 3

Day of German Unity (Germany)

SATURDAY 4

SUNDAY 5

STAR TREK IV: THE VOYAGE HOME

Above: Kirk and Spock travel back in time to locate a pair of humpback whales to repopulate the species on Earth and answer an alien probe.

This film was directed by Leonard Nimoy (Spock), whose work load in the film was hectic.

One of the film sets was the Cetacean aquarium, which was actually part of PARAMOUNT's main parking lot filled with water. This lot also doubled up as San Francisco Bay.

Middle right: following the clash between Kirk and the Klingon Commander Kruge, the Klingon ambassador protests to Starfleet and demands Kirk be punished for his actions.

Below right: The alien probe that was trying to reach the whales in the 24th century. When it could get no response, it started a path of destruction. This prompted Kirk and his crew to come to the rescue, bringing back a pair of humpbacks from the past.

SEPTEMBER						1997	OCTOBER						1997	NOVEMBER						1997
M	T	W	T	F	S	S	M	T	W	T	F	S	S	M	T	W	T	F	S	S
1	2	3	4	5	6	7			1	2	3	4	5						1	2
8	9	10	11	12	13	14	6	7	8	9	10	11	12	3	4	5	6	7	8	9
15	16	17	18	19	20	21	13	14	15	16	17	18	19	10	11	12	13	14	15	16
22	23	24	25	26	27	28	20	21	22	23	24	25	26	17	18	19	20	21	22	23
29	30						27	28	29	30	31			24	25	26	27	28	29	30

OCTOBER

Labour Day (Australia) — **MONDAY 6**

TUESDAY 7

WEDNESDAY 8

THURSDAY 9

Health Sports Day (Taiiku-No-Hi, Japan) — **FRIDAY 10**

Yom Kippur — **SATURDAY 11**

Columbus Day (USA) — **SUNDAY 12**

STAR TREK V: THE FINAL FRONTIER

STAR TREK V: THE FINAL FRONTIER marked the directorial debut of William Shatner (Kirk). As a first time director, he faced many problems, most of which were solved very quickly.

Although the film did not gross as well as expected, it was well-crafted, but had some difficulties in its scripting. That aside, our heroes were shown in yet another light as we learned of their deep and dark pains.

Above: Spock and his brilliant half-brother Sybok. Sybok hijacks the *U.S.S. Enterprise* to take him to where he believes God resides.

Left and right: Kirk is saved by Spock and his jet boots when he falls from the cliff El Capitan during shore leave.

Below: The final destination of Sybok, in search of the mythical 'Sha Ka Ree'.

SEPTEMBER						1997	OCTOBER						1997	NOVEMBER						1997
M	T	W	T	F	S	S	M	T	W	T	F	S	S	M	T	W	T	F	S	S
1	2	3	4	5	6	7			1	2	3	4	5						1	2
8	9	10	11	12	13	14	6	7	8	9	10	11	12	3	4	5	6	7	8	9
15	16	17	18	19	20	21	13	14	15	16	17	18	19	10	11	12	13	14	15	16
22	23	24	25	26	27	28	20	21	22	23	24	25	26	17	18	19	20	21	22	23
29	30						27	28	29	30	31			24	25	26	27	28	29	30

OCTOBER

Columbus Day (USA)
Thanksgiving (Canada)

MONDAY 13

TUESDAY 14

Mark Lenard's Birthday (Ambassador Sarek)

WEDNESDAY 15

THURSDAY 16

FRIDAY 17

SATURDAY 18

SUNDAY 19

STAR TREK VI: THE UNDISCOVERED COUNTRY

Above: Spock's protégé, Valeris (Kim Cattrall), plays a critical role in the film. Apparently there are elements within Starfleet Command that do not approve of the softened stance to the Klingon Empire. They wish to keep hostilities in place and as such, the peace initiatives must be disrupted. Valeris is a sympathiser of this cause, and she sets about to sabotage the Khitomer peace summit.

Below left: Two warriors meet: General Chang and Captain Kirk exchange pleasantries during a social visit by the Klingon leader, Chancellor Gorkon, and his party.

Below right: Valeris shows her true colours as she holds Spock and Kirk at phaser point.

STAR TREK VI: THE UNDISCOVERED COUNTRY, has borrowed its title from a Shakespearean quote which refers to death. This was a prophetic choice of title, as it is the last movie in which the original crew feature as a team. The end of an era, despite the fact that Kirk, Scotty and Chekov make appearances in STAR TREK GENERATIONS.

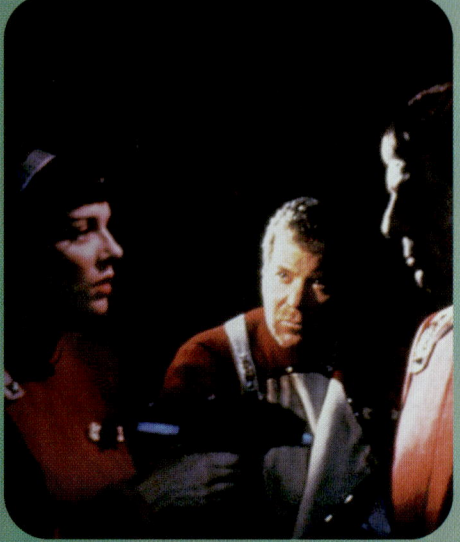

SEPTEMBER					1997			OCTOBER					1997			NOVEMBER					1997	
M	T	W	T	F	S	S		M	T	W	T	F	S	S		M	T	W	T	F	S	S
1	2	3	4	5	6	7				1	2	3	4	5							1	2
8	9	10	11	12	13	14		6	7	8	9	10	11	12		3	4	5	6	7	8	9
15	16	17	18	19	20	21		13	14	15	16	17	18	19		10	11	12	13	14	15	16
22	23	24	25	26	27	28		20	21	22	23	24	25	26		17	18	19	20	21	22	23
29	30							27	28	29	30	31				24	25	26	27	28	29	30

OCTOBER

MONDAY 20

TUESDAY 21

WEDNESDAY 22

THURSDAY 23

United Nations Day

FRIDAY 24

SATURDAY 25

British Summer Time ends

SUNDAY 26

STAR TREK GENERATIONS

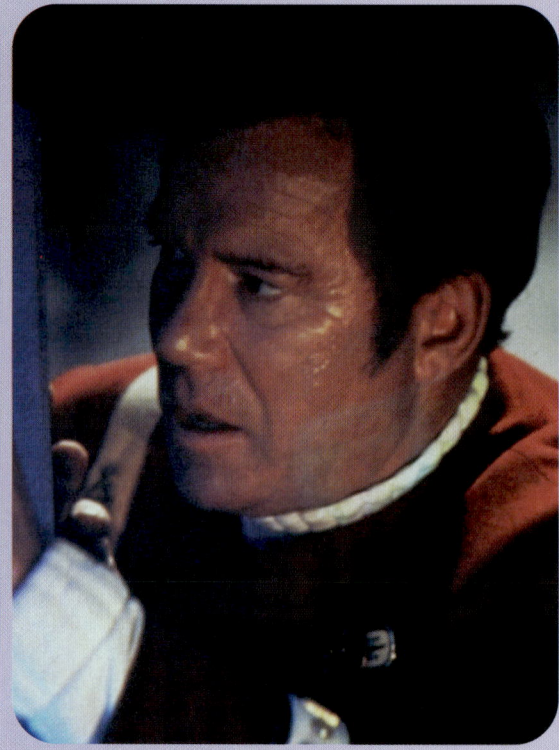

This is the first film to feature the crew from STAR TREK: THE NEXT GENERATION. The scientist Dr Tolian Soran is obsessed with returning to the Nexus. This sets the *U.S.S. Enterprise* on a dangerous journey. Captain Picard (above left) seeks the assistance of Captain Kirk (above right) in the Nexus.

This film is famous for its many deaths, the Duras sisters, Lursa and B'Etor, the *U.S.S. Enterprise*, but most importantly, Captain James T. Kirk.

Below: In American naval costumes, circa 1812, Riker and Deanna participate in the holodeck celebration for the conferring of Lieutenant Worf's new rank of Lieutenant Commander.

OCTOBER						1997	NOVEMBER						1997	DECEMBER						1997
M	T	W	T	F	S	S	M	T	W	T	F	S	S	M	T	W	T	F	S	S
		1	2	3	4	5						1	2	1	2	3	4	5	6	7
6	7	8	9	10	11	12	3	4	5	6	7	8	9	8	9	10	11	12	13	14
13	14	15	16	17	18	19	10	11	12	13	14	15	16	15	16	17	18	19	20	21
20	21	22	23	24	25	26	17	18	19	20	21	22	23	22	23	24	25	26	27	28
27	28	29	30	31			24	25	26	27	28	29	30	29	30	31				

OCTOBER-NOVEMBER

Robert Picardo's Birthday (Emergency Holographic Medical Program)

Holiday (Republic of Ireland)
Labour Day (New Zealand)

MONDAY 27

TUESDAY 28

WEDNESDAY 29

THURSDAY 30

Halloween

FRIDAY 31

All Saints' Day (France, Germany)

SATURDAY 1

SUNDAY 2

STAR TREK GENERATIONS

Above: A desperate Dr Soran holds Captains Kirk and Picard at bay so that he may launch his rocket at the Nexus.

Right: B'Etor taunts Soran, during their brief period of co-operation.

Below: Soran's ultimate aim was to return to the euphoric existence in the Nexus, an energy ribbon in which ultimate fantasies are realised with ease.

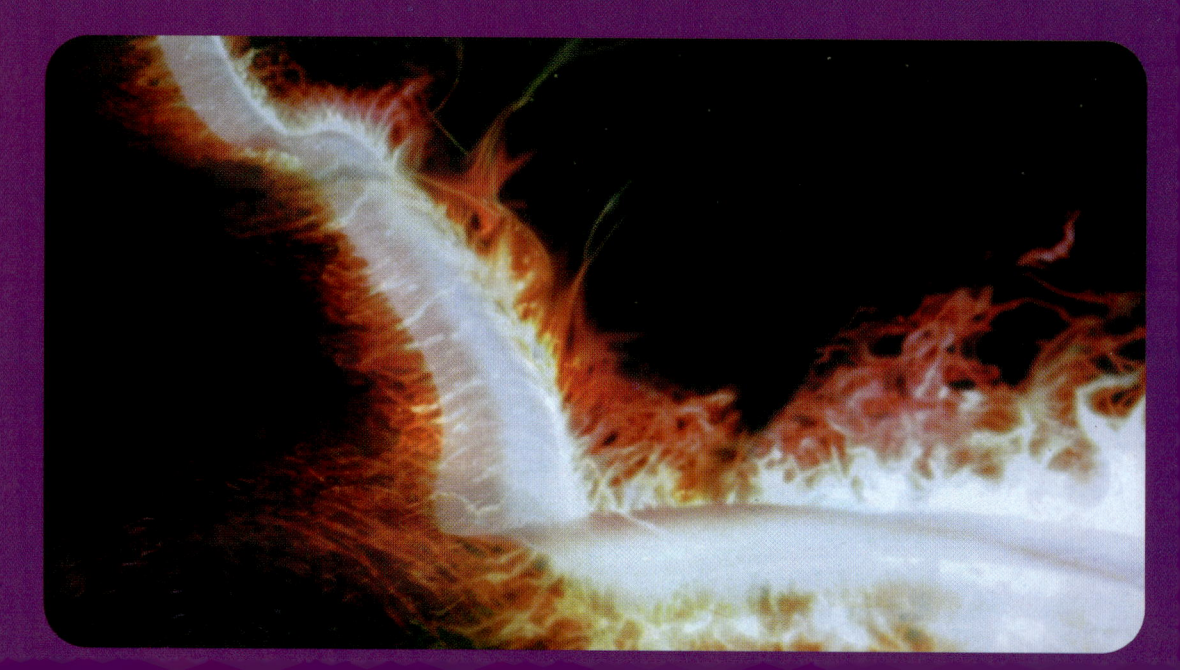

OCTOBER						1997	NOVEMBER						1997	DECEMBER						1997
M	T	W	T	F	S	S	M	T	W	T	F	S	S	M	T	W	T	F	S	S
		1	2	3	4	5						1	2	1	2	3	4	5	6	7
6	7	8	9	10	11	12	3	4	5	6	7	8	9	8	9	10	11	12	13	14
13	14	15	16	17	18	19	10	11	12	13	14	15	16	15	16	17	18	19	20	21
20	21	22	23	24	25	26	17	18	19	20	21	22	23	22	23	24	25	26	27	28
27	28	29	30	31			24	25	26	27	28	29	30	29	30	31				

NOVEMBER

Culture Day (Bunka-No-Hi, Japan)

MONDAY 3

Election Day (USA)
Armin Shimerman's Birthday (Quark)

TUESDAY 4

WEDNESDAY 5

THURSDAY 6

FRIDAY 7

SATURDAY 8

Robert Duncan McNeill's Birthday (Lieutenant Tom Paris)

Remembrance Sunday (UK)

SUNDAY 9

James T. Kirk –
always in command.

OCTOBER						1997	NOVEMBER						1997	DECEMBER						1997
M	T	W	T	F	S	S	M	T	W	T	F	S	S	M	T	W	T	F	S	S
		1	2	3	4	5						1	2	1	2	3	4	5	6	7
6	7	8	9	10	11	12	3	4	5	6	7	8	9	8	9	10	11	12	13	14
13	14	15	16	17	18	19	10	11	12	13	14	15	16	15	16	17	18	19	20	21
20	21	22	23	24	25	26	17	18	19	20	21	22	23	22	23	24	25	26	27	28
27	28	29	30	31			24	25	26	27	28	29	30	29	30	31				

NOVEMBER

MONDAY 10

Armistice Day (1918) (France)
Veteran's Day (USA)
Remembrance Day (Australia)

TUESDAY 11

WEDNESDAY 12

Whoopi Goldberg's Birthday (Guinan)

THURSDAY 13

FRIDAY 14

SATURDAY 15

National Day of Mourning (Germany)

SUNDAY 16

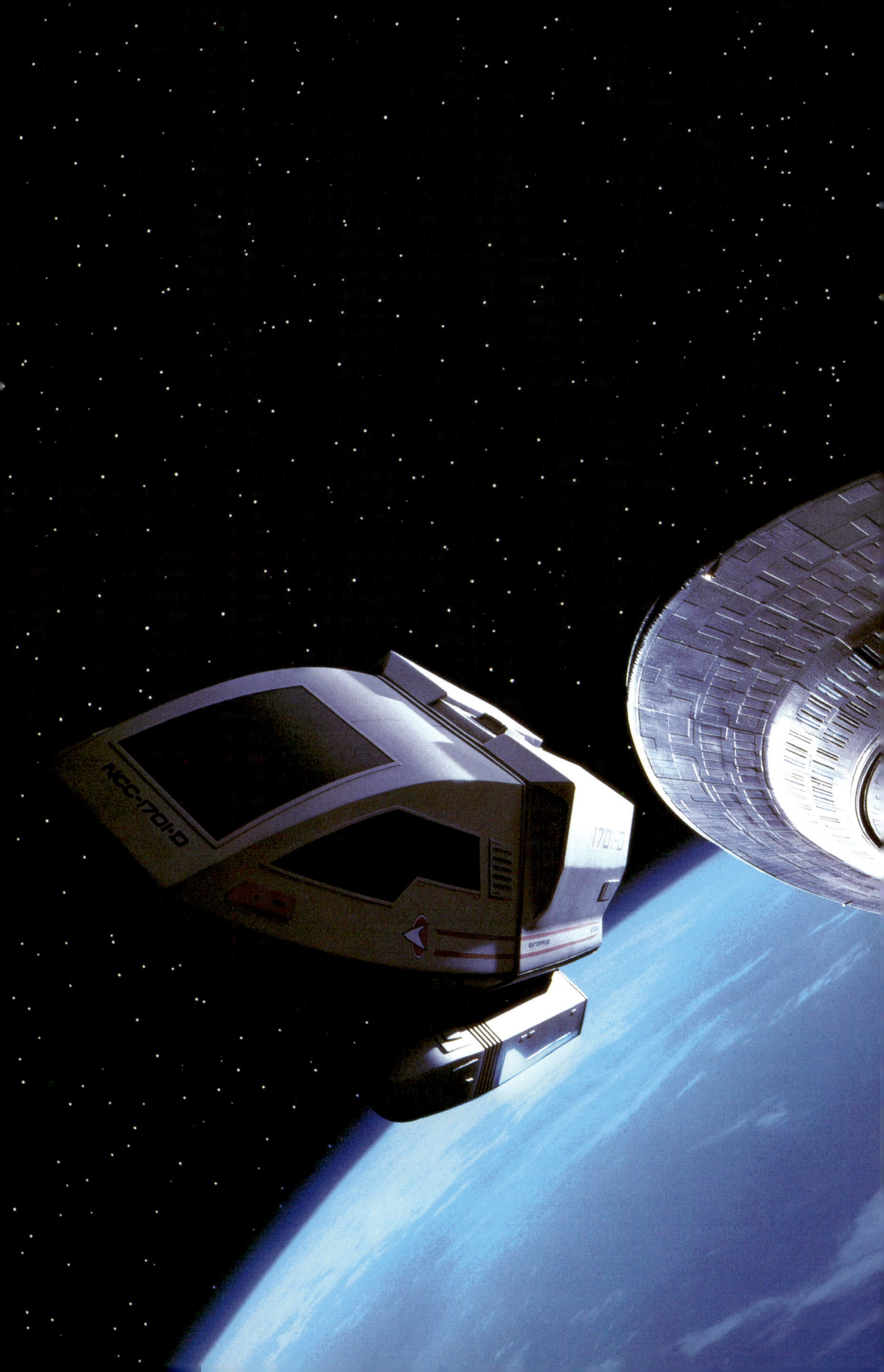
NCC-1701-D
1701-D

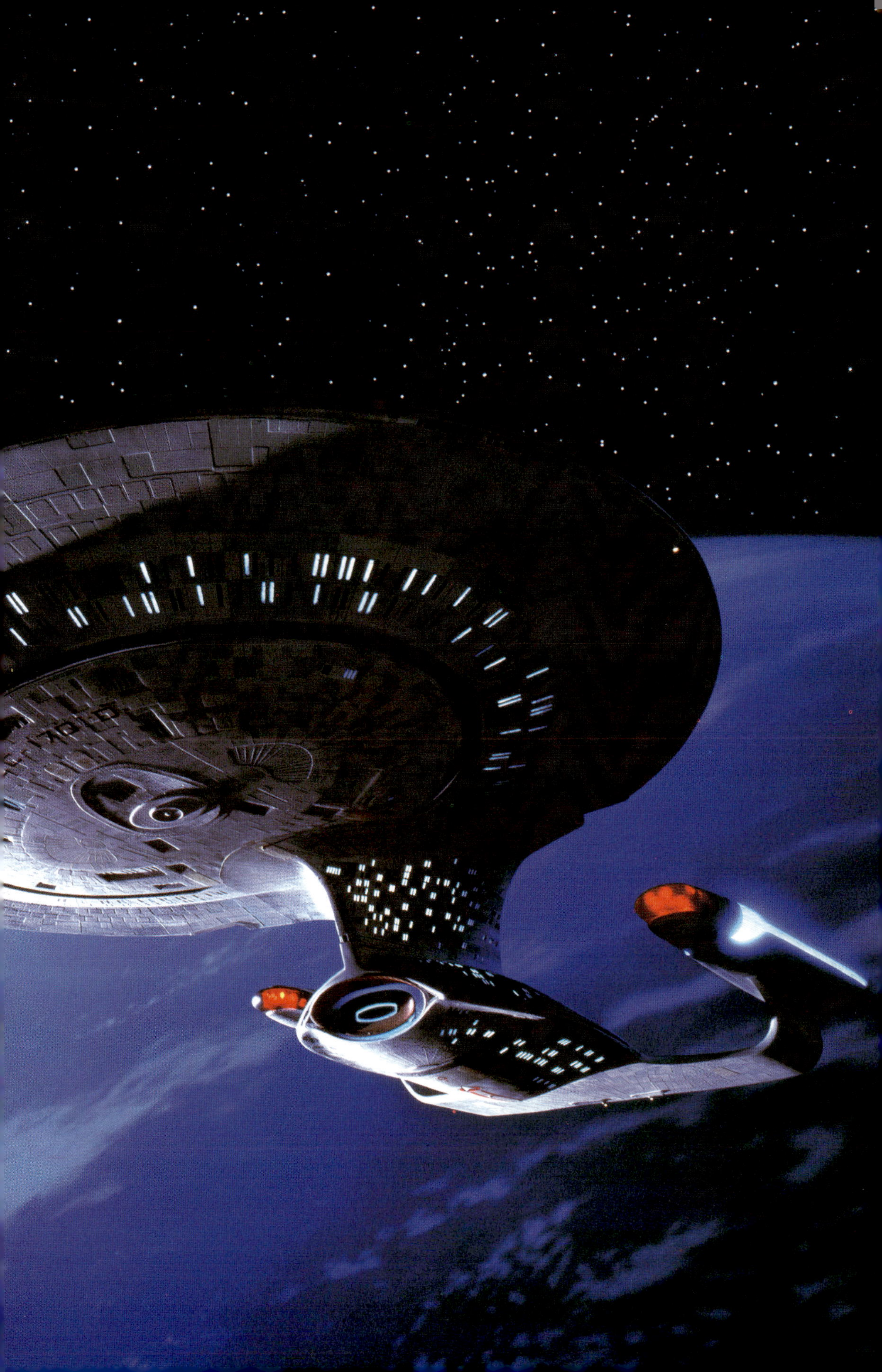

U.S.S. ENTERPRISE NCC-1701

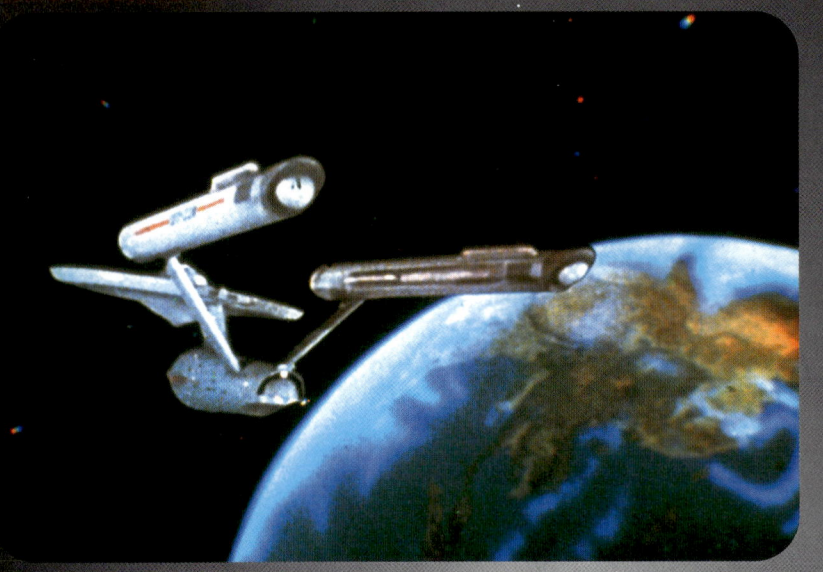

The original *U.S.S. Enterprise* was designed by Art Director "Matt" Jefferies. The design reflected Gene Roddenberry wishes that his starship would not look like the "classic" science fiction ships that came before her. Jefferies's design of the *Enterprise* has set the standard for all starships that have followed.

Below: The ship is trapped in the Tholian web, but manages to break free.

OCTOBER						1997	NOVEMBER						1997	DECEMBER						1997
M	T	W	T	F	S	S	M	T	W	T	F	S	S	M	T	W	T	F	S	S
		1	2	3	4	5						1	2	1	2	3	4	5	6	7
6	7	8	9	10	11	12	3	4	5	6	7	8	9	8	9	10	11	12	13	14
13	14	15	16	17	18	19	10	11	12	13	14	15	16	15	16	17	18	19	20	21
20	21	22	23	24	25	26	17	18	19	20	21	22	23	22	23	24	25	26	27	28
27	28	29	30	31			24	25	26	27	28	29	30	29	30	31				

NOVEMBER

MONDAY 17

TUESDAY 18

Robert Beltran's Birthday (Commander Chakotay)
Terry Farrell's Birthday (Lieutenant Jadzia Dax)

Repentance Day (Germany)

WEDNESDAY 19

THURSDAY 20

FRIDAY 21

Alexander Siddig's Birthday (Dr Julian Bashir)

SATURDAY 22

SUNDAY 23

U.S.S. ENTERPRISE – REFURBISHED

After a year in Spacedock, the *U.S.S. Enterprise* undergoes a full refurbish and refit.

In fact, the *U.S.S. Enterprise* is under the command of Captain Decker until Admiral Kirk takes over in a crisis situation requiring his vast experience.

OCTOBER						1997		NOVEMBER						1997		DECEMBER						1997
M	T	W	T	F	S	S		M	T	W	T	F	S	S		M	T	W	T	F	S	S
		1	2	3	4	5							1	2		1	2	3	4	5	6	7
6	7	8	9	10	11	12		3	4	5	6	7	8	9		8	9	10	11	12	13	14
13	14	15	16	17	18	19		10	11	12	13	14	15	16		15	16	17	18	19	20	21
20	21	22	23	24	25	26		17	18	19	20	21	22	23		22	23	24	25	26	27	28
27	28	29	30	31				24	25	26	27	28	29	30		29	30	31				

NOVEMBER

Denise Crosby's Birthday (Lt Tasha Yar, Sela)

Labour Thanksgiving (Kinro Kansha-No-Hi, Japan)

MONDAY 24

TUESDAY 25

WEDNESDAY 26

Thanksgiving Day (USA)

THURSDAY 27

FRIDAY 28

SATURDAY 29

St Andrew's Day (Scotland)

SUNDAY 30

U.S.S. ENTERPRISE NCC-1701-A

Top: A badly damaged U.S.S. *Enterprise* limps back to Spacedock, after the deadly battle with Khan Noonian Singh in STAR TREK II: THE WRATH OF KHAN.

Below: After saving Earth, Admiral Kirk is reduced in rank to captain. His new command is the U.S.S. *Enterprise* NCC-1701-A.

NOVEMBER						1997		DECEMBER						1997		JANUARY						1998
M	T	W	T	F	S	S		M	T	W	T	F	S	S		M	T	W	T	F	S	S
					1	2		1	2	3	4	5	6	7					1	2	3	4
3	4	5	6	7	8	9		8	9	10	11	12	13	14		5	6	7	8	9	10	11
10	11	12	13	14	15	16		15	16	17	18	19	20	21		12	13	14	15	16	17	18
17	18	19	20	21	22	23		22	23	24	25	26	27	28		19	20	21	22	23	24	25
24	25	26	27	28	29	30		29	30	31						26	27	28	29	30	31	

DECEMBER

MONDAY 1

TUESDAY 2

Brian Bonsall's Birthday (Alexander Roshenko)

WEDNESDAY 3

THURSDAY 4

FRIDAY 5

SATURDAY 6

SUNDAY 7

U.S.S. ENTERPRISE NCC-1701-D

The galaxy class *U.S.S. Enterprise NCC-1701-D* is under the command of Captain Jean-Luc Picard. This huge starship is the latest flagship of the fleet. It has the capacity to carry over 1,000 crew and civilians for extended periods of time.

After the STAR TREK GENERATIONS film, this magnificent design by the Senior Illustrator, Andy Probert, has now passed into history.

NOVEMBER						1997		DECEMBER						1997		JANUARY						1998
M	T	W	T	F	S	S		M	T	W	T	F	S	S		M	T	W	T	F	S	S
					1	2		1	2	3	4	5	6	7					1	2	3	4
3	4	5	6	7	8	9		8	9	10	11	12	13	14		5	6	7	8	9	10	11
10	11	12	13	14	15	16		15	16	17	18	19	20	21		12	13	14	15	16	17	18
17	18	19	20	21	22	23		22	23	24	25	26	27	28		19	20	21	22	23	24	25
24	25	26	27	28	29	30		29	30	31						26	27	28	29	30	31	

DECEMBER

MONDAY 8

Michael Dorn's Birthday (Lieutenant Commander Worf)

TUESDAY 9

WEDNESDAY 10

THURSDAY 11

FRIDAY 12

Garrett Wang's Birthday (Ensign Harry Kim)

SATURDAY 13

SUNDAY 14

U.S.S. DEFIANT

The *U.S.S. Defiant* was added to the arsenal of Space Station *Deep Space 9* in the third season. The new Starship was designed to give the crew manoeuvrability in fighting the Jem'Hadar and guarding against the Dominion.

Braced with advanced, formerly prototype weaponry (including a Romulan Cloaking Device), this Valiant-class ship is more than a match for even the deadliest alien vessel — to date!

In season three, Commander Sisko received a rank promotion to captain of *Deep Space 9* station, one he has carried with great strength.

NOVEMBER						1997		DECEMBER						1997		JANUARY						1998
M	T	W	T	F	S	S		M	T	W	T	F	S	S		M	T	W	T	F	S	S
					1	2		1	2	3	4	5	6	7					1	2	3	4
3	4	5	6	7	8	9		8	9	10	11	12	13	14		5	6	7	8	9	10	11
10	11	12	13	14	15	16		15	16	17	18	19	20	21		12	13	14	15	16	17	18
17	18	19	20	21	22	23		22	23	24	25	26	27	28		19	20	21	22	23	24	25
24	25	26	27	28	29	30		29	30	31						26	27	28	29	30	31	

DECEMBER

MONDAY 15

Reconciliation Day (South Africa)   **TUESDAY 16**

WEDNESDAY 17

THURSDAY 18

FRIDAY 19

SATURDAY 20

SUNDAY 21

U.S.S. VOYAGER

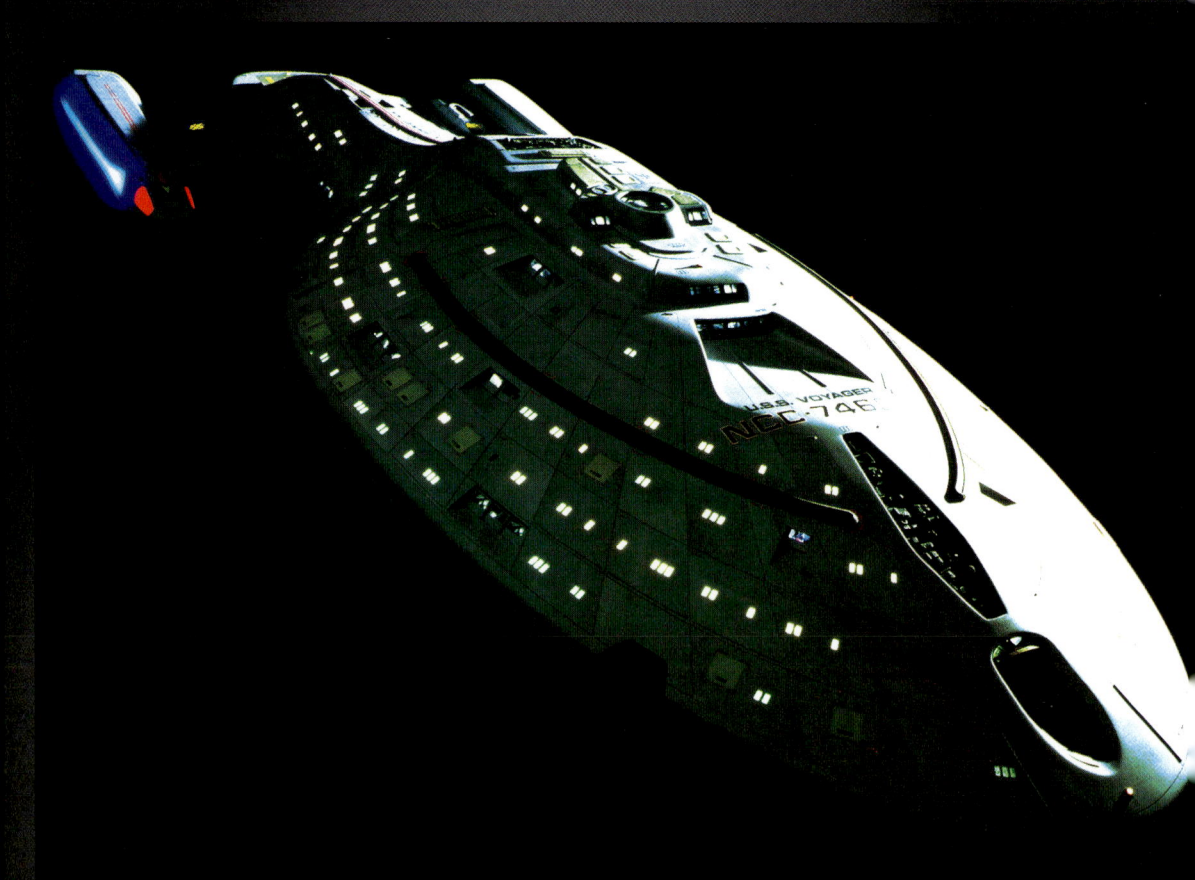

The fourth STAR TREK series, born in 1995, was STAR TREK: VOYAGER, co-created by Rick Berman, Michael Piller and Jeri Taylor.

Featuring all new adventures in the far reaches of the Delta Quadrant. Captain Kathryn Janeway is in command of a brand new ship, the *U.S.S. Voyager*.

Though smaller than a galaxy-class ship, it is every bit as powerful and more manoeuvrable.

NOVEMBER						1997		DECEMBER						1997		JANUARY						1998
M	T	W	T	F	S	S		M	T	W	T	F	S	S		M	T	W	T	F	S	S
					1	2		1	2	3	4	5	6	7					1	2	3	4
3	4	5	6	7	8	9		8	9	10	11	12	13	14		5	6	7	8	9	10	11
10	11	12	13	14	15	16		15	16	17	18	19	20	21		12	13	14	15	16	17	18
17	18	19	20	21	22	23		22	23	24	25	26	27	28		19	20	21	22	23	24	25
24	25	26	27	28	29	30		29	30	31						26	27	28	29	30	31	

DECEMBER

MONDAY 22

Emperor's Birthday (Tenno Tanjo-Bi, Japan)

TUESDAY 23

Christmas Eve
Hanukkah

WEDNESDAY 24

Rick Berman's Birthday (Executive Producer, ST:TNG, ST:DS9, ST:VGR; Co-Creator ST:DS9, ST:VGR; Producer STAR TREK GENERATIONS)

Christmas Day

THURSDAY 25

Boxing Day (St Stephen's Day)
Goodwill Day (South Africa)

FRIDAY 26

SATURDAY 27

Nichelle Nichols' Birthday (Lieutenant Uhura)

SUNDAY 28

SPACE STATION *DEEP SPACE 9*

STAR TREK: DEEP SPACE NINE was conceived in 1993 by Rick Berman and Michael Piller.

They took the bold and unprecendented step to establish an incarnation of STAR TREK using a stationary space station as the focus of activity.

Assembling a strong, well-balanced cast, the show set off to retain the #1 one hour drama show in syndication.

The goal has been achieved, and the intriguing and distinctive design of the station (below) has played a role in this success.

NOVEMBER						1997		DECEMBER						1996		JANUARY						1998
M	T	W	T	F	S	S		M	T	W	T	F	S	S		M	T	W	T	F	S	S
					1	2		1	2	3	4	5	6	7					1	2	3	4
3	4	5	6	7	8	9		8	9	10	11	12	13	14		5	6	7	8	9	10	11
10	11	12	13	14	15	16		15	16	17	18	19	20	21		12	13	14	15	16	17	18
17	18	19	20	21	22	23		22	23	24	25	26	27	28		19	20	21	22	23	24	25
24	25	26	27	28	29	30		29	30	31						26	27	28	29	30	31	

◀ DECEMBER-JANUARY ▶

MONDAY 29

TUESDAY 30

New Year's Eve

WEDNESDAY 31

New Year's Day

THURSDAY 1

FRIDAY 2

SATURDAY 3

SUNDAY 4

OFFICIAL LOG	OFFICIAL LOG
NAME	NAME
ADDRESS	ADDRESS
PH. NO.	PH. NO.
OFFICIAL LOG	OFFICIAL LOG
NAME	NAME
ADDRESS	ADDRESS
PH. NO.	PH. NO.
OFFICIAL LOG	OFFICIAL LOG
NAME	NAME
ADDRESS	ADDRESS
PH. NO.	PH. NO.
OFFICIAL LOG	OFFICIAL LOG
NAME	NAME
ADDRESS	ADDRESS
PH. NO.	PH. NO.
OFFICIAL LOG	OFFICIAL LOG
NAME	NAME
ADDRESS	ADDRESS
PH. NO.	PH. NO.
OFFICIAL LOG	OFFICIAL LOG
NAME	NAME
ADDRESS	ADDRESS
PH. NO.	PH. NO.

OFFICIAL LOG	OFFICIAL LOG
NAME _____ ADDRESS _____ _____ _____ PH. NO. _____	NAME _____ ADDRESS _____ _____ _____ PH. NO. _____
OFFICIAL LOG	OFFICIAL LOG
NAME _____ ADDRESS _____ _____ _____ PH. NO. _____	NAME _____ ADDRESS _____ _____ _____ PH. NO. _____
OFFICIAL LOG	OFFICIAL LOG
NAME _____ ADDRESS _____ _____ _____ PH. NO. _____	NAME _____ ADDRESS _____ _____ _____ PH. NO. _____
OFFICIAL LOG	OFFICIAL LOG
NAME _____ ADDRESS _____ _____ _____ PH. NO. _____	NAME _____ ADDRESS _____ _____ _____ PH. NO. _____
OFFICIAL LOG	OFFICIAL LOG
NAME _____ ADDRESS _____ _____ _____ PH. NO. _____	NAME _____ ADDRESS _____ _____ _____ PH. NO. _____
OFFICIAL LOG	OFFICIAL LOG
NAME _____ ADDRESS _____ _____ _____ PH. NO. _____	NAME _____ ADDRESS _____ _____ _____ PH. NO. _____

OFFICIAL LOG

NAME
ADDRESS

PH. NO.

OFFICIAL LOG

NAME
ADDRESS

PH. NO.

OFFICIAL LOG

NAME
ADDRESS

PH. NO.

OFFICIAL LOG

NAME
ADDRESS

PH. NO.

OFFICIAL LOG

NAME
ADDRESS

PH. NO.

OFFICIAL LOG

NAME
ADDRESS

PH. NO.

OFFICIAL LOG

NAME
ADDRESS

PH. NO.

OFFICIAL LOG

NAME
ADDRESS

PH. NO.

OFFICIAL LOG

NAME
ADDRESS

PH. NO.

OFFICIAL LOG

NAME
ADDRESS

PH. NO.

OFFICIAL LOG

NAME
ADDRESS

PH. NO.

OFFICIAL LOG

NAME
ADDRESS

PH. NO.

OFFICIAL LOG

NAME
ADDRESS
PH. NO.

OFFICIAL LOG

NAME
ADDRESS
PH. NO.

OFFICIAL LOG

NAME
ADDRESS
PH. NO.

OFFICIAL LOG

NAME
ADDRESS
PH. NO.

OFFICIAL LOG

NAME
ADDRESS
PH. NO.

OFFICIAL LOG

NAME
ADDRESS
PH. NO.

OFFICIAL LOG

NAME
ADDRESS
PH. NO.

OFFICIAL LOG

NAME
ADDRESS
PH. NO.

OFFICIAL LOG

NAME
ADDRESS
PH. NO.

OFFICIAL LOG

NAME
ADDRESS
PH. NO.

OFFICIAL LOG

NAME
ADDRESS
PH. NO.

OFFICIAL LOG

NAME
ADDRESS
PH. NO.